Dealing with the Behavioral and Psychological Problems of Students

Ursula Delworth, *Editor*
University of Iowa

NEW DIRECTIONS FOR STUDENT SERVICES

MARGARET J. BARR, *Editor-in-Chief*
Texas Christian University

M. LEE UPCRAFT, *Associate Editor*
Pennsylvania State University

Number 45, Spring 1989

Paperback sourcebooks in
The Jossey-Bass Higher Education Series

Jossey-Bass Inc., Publishers
San Francisco • London

Ursula Delworth (ed.).
Dealing with the Behavioral and Psychological Problems of Students.
New Directions for Student Services, no. 45.
San Francisco: Jossey-Bass, 1989.

New Directions for Student Services
Margaret J. Barr, *Editor-in-Chief;* M. Lee Upcraft, *Associate Editor*

New Directions for Student Services is published quarterly
by Jossey-Bass Inc., Publishers (publication number USPS
449-070). Second-class postage paid at San Francisco, California, and
at additional mailing offices. POSTMASTER: Send address changes
to Jossey-Bass Inc., Publishers, 350 Sansome Street, San Francisco,
California 94104.

Editorial correspondence should be sent to the Editor-in-Chief,
Margaret J. Barr, Sadler Hall, Texas Christian University,
Fort Worth, Texas 76129.

Library of Congress Catalog Card Number LC 85-644751

International Standard Serial Number ISSN 0164-7970

International Standard Book Number ISBN 1-55542-876-2

Cover art by WILLI BAUM

Manufactured in the United States of America. Printed on acid-free paper.

Ordering Information

The paperback sourcebooks listed below are published quarterly and can be ordered either by subscription or single copy.

Subscriptions cost $52.00 per year for institutions, agencies, and libraries. Individuals can subscribe at the special rate of $39.00 per year *if payment is by personal check.* (Note that the full rate of $52.00 applies if payment is by institutional check, even if the subscription is designated for an individual.) Standing orders are accepted.

Single copies are available at $12.95 when payment accompanies order. (California, New Jersey, New York, and Washington, D.C., residents please include appropriate sales tax.) For billed orders, cost per copy is $12.95 plus postage and handling.

Substantial discounts are offered to organizations and individuals wishing to purchase bulk quantities of Jossey-Bass sourcebooks. Please inquire.

Please note that these prices are for the calendar year 1989 and are subject to change without notice. Also, some titles may be out of print and therefore not available for sale.

To ensure correct and prompt delivery, all orders must give either the *name of an individual* or an *official purchase order number.* Please submit your order as follows:

Subscriptions: specify series and year subscription is to begin.
Single Copies: specify sourcebook code (such as, SS1) and first two words of title.

Mail orders for United States and Possessions, Latin America, Canada, Japan, Australia, and New Zealand to:
Jossey-Bass Inc., Publishers
350 Sansome Street
San Francisco, California 94104

Mail orders for all other parts of the world to:
Jossey-Bass Limited
28 Banner Street
London EC1Y 8QE

New Directions for Student Services Series
Margaret J. Barr, *Editor-in-Chief;* M. Lee Upcraft, *Associate Editor*

Contents

Editor's Notes

In my more despairing moments, it seems to me that the modern university has succeeded in separating almost everything that belongs together.
Nevitt Sanford, 1982

Those of us who work on campus with a larger array of problematic student behaviors often find ourselves echoing these words, though they were originally spoken in another context. Theory and procedures rarely mesh, and our own intuitive sense fails us as we attempt to both understand the students with whom we work and aid them in their quests for maturity and achievement.

There are, of course, no easy answers. My hope is that the Assessment-Intervention of Student Problems (AISP) model will move us along the path toward more effective and efficient work with students. This model was first conceived when Chicagoland (Illinois) Deans requested help with coordinating student services and psychological perspectives in order to cope with problem students. The encouragement I received from these deans, and in subsequent presentations, led me to accept an invitation to edit this volume of New Directions for Student Services.

The AISP model presents an integrative stance regarding students with problems. The model is explicit in holding that members of the student services staff, along with other key members of the campus community, must work in an integrated, systematic way to ensure effective and just treatment of students who exhibit dysfunctional behavior. Included in the model are three key elements: the assessment of students, the campus intervention team, and the interventions.

The model divides students into three general categories: disturbing, disturbed, and disturbed/disturbing. The first group (disturbing students) is composed of students who cause problems in the campus environment. They tend to be immature and manipulative and to have difficulties with many aspects of college life. Disturbed students are those who exhibit marked patterns of behavior that are "out of sync" with peers and generally accepted norms. Their own inner turmoil poses problems for them in adjusting to and achieving in the college environment. Disturbed/disturbing students are those who demonstrate behaviors that are problems both for themselves and for the institution, and both patterns are sufficiently severe to warrant assessment and intervention.

1

A campus intervention team is proposed in this model as the primary system component to set or approve policy and procedures and to coordinate assessment of and interventions with students. Interventions include both those that can be implemented through campus and community structures, and those that require removal of the students from the campus environment.

The AISP model is helpful to student services professionals and administrators in several ways. First, it provides coordination and direction in efforts to both help students and maintain an orderly and healthy environment on campus. It demystifies issues of student assessment for staff members who do not possess formal training in these areas. In addition, it provides a common language and a support system for staff members who are dealing with difficult issues.

In the first chapter, I present the AISP model in some detail. In Chapter Two, Ragle and Justice speak specifically to issues that deal with disturbing students. McKinley and Dworkin, in Chapter Three, discuss disturbed students. And Brown and DeCoster devote Chapter Four to the study of disturbed/disturbing students. In Chapter Five, Sandeen, an experienced chief student affairs officer, shares his perspective and critique of the model. Shang, Rhatigan, and Eklund-Leen examine the model in terms of more diverse populations in Chapters Six, Seven, and Eight.

This volume of New Directions for Student Services is designed for practitioners of all types and levels. We hope it will be of service to you in your struggle to understand and help the diverse students with whom you work.

Ursula Delworth
Editor

Reference

Sanford, N. "Foreword." In J. Whiteley (ed.), *Character Development in College Students.* Schenectady, N.Y.: Character Research Press, 1982.

Ursula Delworth is a student affairs professional and psychologist. She is currently a professor in the Department of Psychological and Quantitative Foundations of Education, The University of Iowa.

The Assessment-Intervention of Student Problems model provides a comprehensive process for understanding and helping students who are either having problems themselves or are causing problems for others on campus.

The AISP Model: Assessment-Intervention of Student Problems

Ursula Delworth

Case example: Jane was a very quiet freshman in the residence hall, one who slipped between the cracks. However, late in the fall semester, her roommate and two other women from her floor talked with their resident assistant about their concerns for Jane. They reported that she sat for hours staring into space, had frequent unexplained crying spells, and was not attending classes regularly. She refused to discuss her problems with any of them and often would not speak to them at all.

Case example: John was a freshman who was noticed from the first day he arrived on campus. Within days, he was in trouble for playing unappreciated pranks on his roommates, for raucous behavior in the dining hall, and for violating the hall's alcohol policy. When confronted by his roommates and staff members on these issues, John was at first belligerent, and then contrite. However, problems persisted during the first month of the semester.

Case example: Jake, a junior living off campus, has repeatedly called campus security and city police, complaining of nocturnal attacks by an unknown enemy. Jake also complained to the dean of students that he could not study or attend classes because he was so upset and tired from lack of sleep.

U. Delworth (ed.). *Dealing with the Behavioral and Psychological Problems of Students.*
New Directions for Student Services, no. 45. San Francisco: Jossey-Bass, Spring 1989.

Students like Jane, John, and Jake are familiar to every student services professional. The question becomes: How do we help the student and at the same time provide an appropriate environment on campus? This is no easy set of tasks, most especially for younger workers just starting out in the field, and for residence hall staff, many of whom are students themselves. It is often unclear when psychological or disciplinary resources are needed, or when both are required. Often, staff members feel isolated and confused in dealing with such situations, and they end up feeling ineffective.

Such situations require clear procedures for assessing the student and for moving the student into the appropriate system for further assessment and intervention. The AISP, or Assessment-Intervention of Student Problems model, proposes guidelines for such procedures. Though no system is simple or foolproof, the AISP model has the advantages of involving a diversity of relevant campus professionals and of being relatively easy to understand. Within its guidelines, procedures can be developed to match the needs and resources of specific campuses.

There are three parts to the model: the assessment of the student, the campus intervention team, and the intervention. Though all are essential, the main focus is on the first part, assessment of the student, because general assessment of student problems is a responsibility for all staff members, whereas the campus intervention team and intervention skills tend to be the prime responsibility of the supervisory and administrative staff. All, however, are discussed in this chapter, and they are discussed in more detail in subsequent chapters.

The Student

The first step in using the AISP model is to develop a general assessment of the student, so that assignment to the appropriate system can be made. Though this assessment procedure is admittedly somewhat simplistic, it nevertheless serves a useful purpose, allowing staff members to make appropriate decisions regarding more specific assessment and intervention. It has the advantage of covering a wide range of student problems. In addition, it is straightforward and rather easily learned by novice staff members. Both experienced and new staff members can benefit from the support, confirmation, and follow-through provided in this model.

The model divides students into three general categories: the disturbing student, the disturbed student, and the disturbed/disturbing student. Each will be discussed in turn. Exhibit 1 presents an outline of the categories.

The Disturbing Student. This student demonstrates a lack of skills in establishing close, age-appropriate relationships. He or she is quite self-centered but wants to establish relationships with others. Two types of

Exhibit 1. Assessment Categories of Problem Students

I. The Disturbing Student
Description: Lacks skills in establishing close, age-appropriate relationships; very self-centered but wants to establish relationships.

Type A: Immature
  - Shows immature reactions to many aspects of college life
  - Plays pranks
  - Does not respect property of others
  - Overreacts to minor problems
  - May abuse alcohol
  - Gets angry and upset easily
  - Has low frustration tolerance
  - Engages in illegal activities that tend to be overt (for example, disorderly conduct).

Type B: Con Artist
  - Wants to manipulate and control
  - Tests limits
  - Usually can be charming
  - Engages in illegal activities that tend to be covert (for example, drug dealing)
  - May abuse alcohol or illegal substances or both.

II. The Disturbed Student
Description: Specific behaviors and patterns of behavior are out of sync with other students; often marked patterns of moving away from *or* against others; may overly fixate on one goal or idea; may evince overall rigid, highly dualistic thinking; may make inappropriate or off-task remarks; seems angry and destructive toward self or others.

Type A: Inward Focus
  - Depressed, withdrawn—perhaps to the point of being suicidal
  - Little involvement in classes and campus life.

Type B: Outward Focus
  - Angry at world and particular persons—perhaps to the point of being homicidal
  - May be involved, but with less frequency, with "mainstream" groups.

A-B 1: Symptoms are recent; following known precipitating cause
A-B 2: Symptoms are recent; no known cause
A-B 3: Symptoms are long-standing; no real change
A-B 4: Symptoms are long-standing; worsening after period of better adjustment
A-B 5: Symptoms are long-standing; worsening steadily.

III. The Disturbed/Disturbing Student
Description: Any combinations of I and II are possible. Some typical combinations:

1. Student is *disturbing* residence hall and campus security with stories of being attacked in his or her residence-hall room every night by an enemy (or any other persistent and illogical complaint), thus evincing *disturbed* behavior.
2. Student is depressed and withdrawn (*disturbed*) except when drinking. Student then picks fights, destroys residence-hall property, and so on (*disturbing*).
3. Student misuses financial aid (*disturbing*) in order to pay for a medical operation on a disorder that physicians cannot verify, thus evincing *disturbed* behavior.
4. Student is *disturbing* residence-hall floor by threatening to commit suicide, following the death of a close relative (*disturbed*).

these students can be identified. Type A disturbing students are character-ized by an overall immaturity that makes it difficult for them to function appropriately in the college environment. They have difficulty with many aspects of college life. In the residence halls, they often indicate disrespect for the property of others, play "pranks," and may abuse alcohol. In their academic work, they show low frustration tolerance and may often drop classes that demand a high degree of sustained effort. They tend to overreact to minor difficulties, and their illegal activities (if any) are usually in the area of disorderly conduct. Overall, they give the impres-sion of not being mature enough to handle the college or university environment.

Case example: John fit into this category. Coming from a small rural high school, and being the youngest in a large family, his role as clown had earned him a place at home. He had escaped many of the responsi-bilities his older siblings assumed, and his high intelligence allowed him to do well academically without much effort. In the relatively impersonal environment of a large state university, John felt that "nobody knows my name." He set out to make friends by using behaviors that were successful within his family, but they were not well regarded by others in his new environment. He thus found himself frustrated and confused and also "stuck" in old behavior patterns.

Type B disturbing students tend to be much more controlling and manipulative. They have learned to get their way by testing the limits in each environment and then using "charm" to attempt to escape conse-quences of their behavior. They are often not as frustrating to staff and faculty members as the type A students are, since they know better how far to push limits, and they have better interpersonal skills. However, they are the con artists of the campus, and they are more likely than type A students to violate the law. They may become drug dealers or abusers or both.

Case example: Jolene was an example of a type B disturbing student. Coming from a wealthy family, she had learned at an early age to manip-ulate her parents into giving her everything she wanted. At college, she wanted to do as little work as possible to pass her courses, and she tried to control friends through her charm and extravagant gifts. By her senior year, she was an aimless, academically borderline student, dealing drugs to finance her own drug problem along with a lifestyle beyond that which her parents were able to provide. She was finally arrested for sell-ing drugs.

Of course, it is entirely possible for a disturbing student to have char-acteristics of both type A and type B. These students may also have some problems that could benefit from psychological intervention. Their deter-minining characteristic, however, is that they are *disturbing* the campus environment and do not have clear signs of serious psychological disturbance, although it is clear that they are experiencing some difficulties of a psychological nature. Their disturbing behavior tends to be chronic. That is, they tend not to learn from experience, and they have a difficult time settling into the college community. Many tend toward major disturbances, such as involvement in illegal activities.

The Disturbed Student. These students exhibit specific behaviors and patterns of behavior that are out of sync with other students and are often marked by a moving away from or setting themselves against others. They not only lack a sense of how to establish positive interpersonal relationships but they may also have no interest in doing so. In some cases, they may not believe such relationships are possible. They evince a wide variety of behaviors. In some cases they are unusually withdrawn. In others, they are overly fixated on one goal or idea and demonstrate overly rigid, highly dualistic thinking. They may make inappropriate or off-task remarks in classrooms and other settings. Often, they appear angry and destructive toward themselves or others, and in some cases, they make suicidal gestures. At the extreme, they may carry out suicide threats.

This group can also be divided into types. Type A disturbed students have an inward focus. They are depressed and withdrawn and are more likely to evince suicidal ideation or gestures. They are minimally involved in their course work and other aspects of student life.

Case example: Jane was a type A disturbed student. She had been treated for depression in junior high school, after the suicide of her older brother, who had been a college student at the time. She had made adequate social and good academic adjustment in high school but was not able to remain adjusted after entering the new college environment and approaching the age at which her brother had died (nineteen). Though not overtly suicidal, she had increasingly been disengaging herself from significant life tasks and experiences.

The type B disturbed student maintains an outward focus, angry at the world and particular persons. He or she may be engaged in academics, but only those courses that allow the basic angry stance to be expressed in some way. More typically, this student feels alienated from academics, and "mainstream" activities but may be involved in groups that are working toward a change in the system. The problems of this student, however, are too intense to allow organized, systematic efforts toward a group goal, so he or she remains a fringe member of the group.

Case example: Jason was such a student. He lived in a room off campus, had been in and out of school, and had taken part in rallies on peace and environmental causes, where he could rant about the "establishment." Near the point of being expelled from the college because he had not made sufficient academic progress, he claimed that "they" (all campus and societal forces) were out to get him and expressed particular anger toward the dean of students. Jason had a history of aggressive behavior, beginning in elementary school, but had no criminal record. Though he was considered a nuisance on campus, he was not seen as a serious threat. From time to time, he dropped out of activities to talk to his "demons."

It is possible for type A and type B behaviors to overlap, but this is unusual. The dynamics of individual pathology are such that the student's overall focus is almost always turned either inward or outward. Beneath the surface, of course, the opposite focus is often present. Jason, for example, carried a heavy load of self-hatred, and Jane was angry at both the brother who deserted her and the parents whom she felt had let him down. Disturbed students, of course, can cause some minor "disturbances" in the system. But they are easily identified as being a problem primarily to themselves.

Both types of disturbed students must be assessed in terms of the duration and cause of their symptoms. When possible and feasible, the student services professional can help with this process. Often, it is necessary for a member of the campus mental health system to complete the process. The assessment is important because duration of problems is an important indicator of appropriate intervention, and often student services administrators must take it into consideration when determining whether to suspend or expel the student.

In evaluating duration, the problems that are recent and have a known cause carry the best prognosis for treatment in the campus environment, and for full recovery. Many of these are more serious problems of a developmental nature and are further addressed in Chapters Three and Four of this issue. Problems having a longer duration, such as those of Jason and Jane, are somewhat less promising. A method of categorizing these variables is given in the second section of Exhibit 1.

In this system, Jane would be seen as an A-4. Her symptoms have worsened, but she had made and maintained an adequate adjustment in high school. Jason, however, would be a B-5. His problems are chronic, but they have worsened, in that he was in danger of academic dismissal, and he was generally more interpersonally isolated than at previous periods in his life.

The Disturbed/Disturbing Student. For this student, any combination of disturbing and disturbed behaviors is possible. The key in assessment is that both aspects are prominent enough to require referral and intervention. If one aspect is less prominent, this classification should not be utilized. For example, John may well have been able to use some social-skills counseling, but his disturbing behavior was the prime focus. Jason's behavior almost became disturbing to the campus environment, but so far these problems were minor, and the focus was on his individual disturbance.

Case example: Jake provides a good example of a disturbed/disturbing student. His unverified fears of an unknown enemy indicated psychological disturbance and should be addressed. At the same time, his undue burdening of law enforcement resources was disturbing and unacceptable and must therefore be addressed as well.

Other common examples of disturbed/disturbing students are presented in Exhibit 1. Again, the assessment for this category is made when both sets of behaviors are sufficiently overt to be prime focuses for further assessment and intervention.

Assessment Process. The process of making an appropriate general assessment and choosing one of these categories depends to some extent on the role of the assessor. Often a supervisor or administrator must gather appropriate data from several sources in order to complete this task. Many times, disturbing behavior is observed more readily by residence-hall or law enforcement personnel. Faculty members, employers, or other students may be the first to observe disturbed behavior. Thus, besides interviewing the student and talking with the first person or persons to report the behavior, staff members should consult with other relevant sources. In many cases, this is the responsibility of the staff member's supervisor. Also, it is important to follow institutional policies both when requesting and when sharing information. Especially when considering making an assessment of a disturbed/disturbing student, it may be appropriate to hold a meeting with all relevant information sources, including the student. The point of this general preliminary assessment is to refer the student to the appropriate agency or agencies within the campus or larger community.

The Campus Intervention Team

All campuses have or should have some system in place for handling the discipline or judicial problems and the psychological problems of students. The issue often becomes one of insufficient coordination, inadequate information flow, and lack of a shared process. Therefore, a coordinated system is an essential component in the AISP mode. The group responsible for such coordination is usually termed campus intervention team, but is equally effective by any other name and is the mechanism to make certain that all systems work effectively, and to aid them in so doing. The team is minimally composed of key personnel from (1) campus mental health services, (2) campus security, (3) the student services administration, (4) the institution's legal counselors, and (5) the student services judicial or discipline office. Other relevant persons can be included on a permanent basis, or included as needed for a specific issue, which will help to keep the group at a smaller, more functional size. (See also chapters Six, Seven, and Eight of this volume.)

The responsibilities of the team are several. First, the team should help develop (or at least approve) policies and procedures to assess students and to assign them to specific systems within the institution. Second, the team should be kept apprised of such assignments. The third and most time-consuming function of the team is to develop and implement assessment and intervention programs for students who are either initially assessed as disturbed/disturbing or do not profit from initial assignments. On many campuses, the team also assumes responsibility for educating staff members about relevant policies and procedures.

Figure 1 indicates the kind of communication and responsibility flow that should be expected by the team. The majority of student problems should be handled through either the judicial or the mental health systems, and the team's involvement should be restricted to setting or approving policies and procedures.

The team may function either as a decision-making group or as an advisory group to relevant decision makers (who vary from situation to situation). Since some decisions, such as involuntary withdrawal, are almost always assigned to a specific administrator, the team needs to play at least an advisory role in such cases. Often members of the team, and sometimes the entire team, function as a primary source of information and support for frontline staff and family members and friends of students. This requires that the team be sensitive both to legitimate needs for information and to clear guidelines for confidentiality.

In this model, assessments of disturbed students assume that a referral to the mental health system will be made, either on campus or in the community. Assessments of disturbing students assume referral to the appropriate judicial system. In many cases, this can be accomplished in an expeditious and effective manner. However, problems do arise. In particular, referrals to the mental health system may not be accepted by a disturbed student, who either sees no problem with his or her behavior, or lacks energy and motivation for change. The team should be closely involved in these cases, making sure that set procedures are followed and determining courses of action for individual cases.

Thus John was directly referred to the judicial system, and Jolene was referred after her arrest. Jane accepted a referral to the mental health system (counseling center) with the help of her roommate and the resident assistant. Jason refused help and dropped out of school but returned later and was flagged for an intervention plan by the team. Jake's situation was handled initially through the team, whose subsequent plan contained two components: a behavioral contract regarding calls to police, which was monitored through the judicial system, and referral to the counseling center, which resulted in a brief psychiatric hospitalization and ongoing outpatient treatment and monitoring of medication.

In some instances, an appropriate referral to one system at one point

Figure 1. The Student, the System, and Interventions

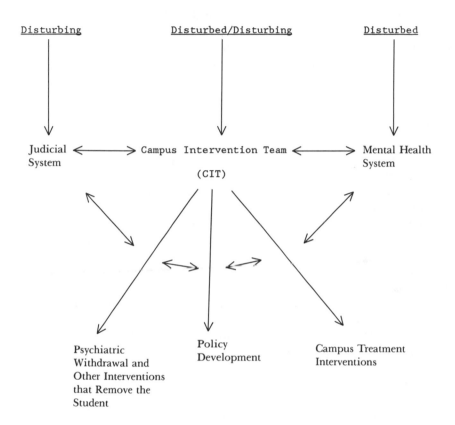

in time may become outdated and require an additional referral and intervention at another. For example, John did alter his behavior as a result of actions in the judicial system, but then became depressed because he did not have appropriate relationship skills. It was important for the team to trace his progress to ensure that an appropriate counseling referral was made.

As might be implied from this discussion, this model assumes a considerable commitment of time and energy from the team. Both regular and emergency meetings are part of the job, although some situations can clearly be handled by telephone conversations among team members. The benefit of this model is a system that works, both for the student and for more broad institutional interests.

At this point, it makes sense to turn to the third portion of the model, that of interventions. As Figure 1 indicates, many problems are handled effectively within the traditional services of the judicial and mental health systems. Most are handled in this manner. The focus here is on those situations in which a multidimensional approach is indicated, and in which the campus intervention team must play a vital role.

Interventions

Two major types of interventions are appropriate for discussion here. The first includes all those interventions through which the student is either willingly or unwillingly removed from the campus environment. The second type includes all the interventions possible while letting the student remain enrolled, regardless of whether these interventions occur through campus or community agencies.

Removal Interventions. The student may, of course, simply decide to withdraw from the institution, or he or she may be removed by law enforcement agencies for such purposes as serving a jail term. Beyond these possibilities, the most common removal interventions are initiated by the institution for reasons having to do with academic performance, conduct, or psychiatric problems. Whenever one of these actions is seriously considered, the campus team and student services administrators must be sure that the action clearly follows established policy and procedures and that it upholds due-process rights. Presumably, other avenues are carefully explored before this decision is made. In the case of psychiatric withdrawal, it must be clear that the unacceptable conduct occurred as a result of a mental disorder or defect. Though unfortunate, removal of the student is sometimes the only viable alternative that will ensure individual safety and prevent continued disruptions. (See Chapter Four of this volume for a more detailed discussion of this intervention.)

Campus Interventions. This discussion focuses on disturbing students who are referred to the judicial system, disturbed students who are referred to the mental health system, and disturbed/disturbing students who are referred to both systems. Some of the interventions are likely to occur within these two major systems. The judicial system sets up penalties for inappropriate behavior and enforces its standards in this regard. (See Chapter Two of this volume.) Mental health interventions help the student explore his or her personal history and old patterns and develop new ways of coping in the environment. (See Chapter Three of this volume.) Sadly, however, these interventions are often less than optimally effective because they occur in isolation and do not become integrated with the student's day-to-day life. One of the responsibilities of the campus intervention team is to work toward a more integrated plan of interventions, which will help the student become successfully integrated into the campus community. These interventions can be part of the judicial process or mental health treatment, or they may occur in conjunction with those approaches.

Two major intervention areas are important when considering disturbing, disturbed, or disturbed/disturbing students. The first is the social/interpersonal intervention, which involves facilitating a bonding, or sense of connection, with one or more persons in the campus community. Specific interventions include membership in a support group or campus activity and mentoring by an appropriate older student, faculty member, or staff member. For example, Jane was able to join a support group of students who had experienced a death in their family, and here she opened up to peers for the first time. John became involved in one of the committees planning the campus homecoming celebration and here he learned to take responsibility for his work and also made several good friends. Jake, after a period of intensive individual treatment, joined a therapy group and was able to share an apartment with two roommates. Living with others helped him overcome his extreme isolation and provided some regular interpersonal interaction. Jolene, following substance abuse treatment, joined a support group for women with substance abuse problems, and she also joined the technical crew for campus theater productions. Here she found a faculty member in the theater department who became her academic adviser and mentor, and who was helpful in introducing Jolene to a new set of values so that she began to place less importance on material possessions.

A second area of interventions deals with skills and competencies. Students in all three of our categories experience some sort of skills deficits as they attempt to adjust to the college or university environment. Common skills that these students need are (1) academic and study skills, (2) career decision-making skills, (3) interpersonal skills, and (4) behavioral coping skills. Some students also benefit from anxiety-reduction training, assertion training, and financial management training. Jolene, for example, used financial management training to become more independent of her parents and learn to live within her income. John benefited from study skills training, and both Jane and Jake joined a social skills training group. Jason, on his return to college, completed both the study skills and the career decision-making groups.

In some instances, students find these interpersonal and skills-enhancing interventions on their own. However, that is not often the case. The campus team, or some subset of its members, needs to fill the role of temporary significant other for the student as he or she struggles to find a place in the campus environment. Especially on larger campuses, this is not likely to happen by accident, yet often these interventions are essential to the full of engagement of the student and to the maximization of what he or she gains from the college experience.

Caveats and Conclusion

As presented here, the AISP model appears more linear and simplistic than it is in reality. Students do not always remain in the categories they were originally assigned to. The best-laid plans of a team can go awry. And sometimes no amount of effort seems to make a difference. Then, too, we have focused on traditional-aged college students in developing this model. How does it work with such groups as ethnic minorities, athletes, and commuter students? These questions are addressed in chapters Six, Seven, and Eight by professionals with expertise in these areas. Chapters Two through Five address the model in more detail, from the perspectives of experienced administrators.

Student services professionals must be able to perform general assessment of student problems and make appropriate referrals. They have the right to expect the kind of support and structure offered by some form of campus intervention team. Working together, the professional and the team can be of significant help to students. It is hoped that the AISP model will be a useful tool in making the task both easier and more effective.

Ursula Delworth is former coeditor of New Directions for Student Services, *coeditor of* Student Services: A Handbook for the Profession, *and a recipient of the Contribution to Knowledge Award of the American College Personnel Association.*

In the context of a larger system such as the Assessment-
Intervention of Student Problems model, the judicial process
can respond to the disturbing student in a manner that is
constructive for the student as well as for the institution.

The Disturbing Student and the Judicial Process

John D. Ragle, Sharon H. Justice

The Assessment-Intervention of Student Problems (AISP) model is a useful tool for preparing student services professionals to assess the problems of disturbed, disturbing, or disturbed/disturbing students and to make appropriate referrals. It is particularly useful because it emphasizes the necessity of developing an integrated *system* for this assessment and referral process, a system that includes staff members who are prepared to deal with psychological, disciplinary, legal, and campus security aspects of a problem student's situation. In the past, the disturbing student has been too often solely the purview of the "discipline officer"—a single member of the student services staff who investigates complaints, metes out punishment, and counsels offending students in relative isolation. Other professionals have tended to view the work of the disciplinarian as a necessary but unappealing aspect of the student services profession. Such an isolated system has limited the possible benefits available both to students and to the institution from the constructive resolution of a disturbing student's problems.

As Delworth points out in Chapter One of this volume, disturbing students are usually either immature and impulsive (type A) or controlling and manipulative (type B). They act out in a variety of ways, running afoul of the accepted standards of behavior in a university

U. Delworth (ed.). *Dealing with the Behavioral and Psychological Problems of Students.*
New Directions for Student Services, no. 45. San Francisco: Jossey-Bass, Spring 1989.

community both inside and outside the classroom. Sometimes the misbehavior is amusingly naive or inventive: the art student who decides to use a university kiln to cremate his beloved pet (deceased) and to serve alcohol at the wake, or the group of freshmen who go out to steal a campus stop sign and ask a nearby maintenance worker if they can borrow his tools. But sometimes the misbehavior is disruptive to the effective functioning of an educational institution: the student who dyes and perms his hair to disguise himself in order to take a placement test for a friend, the student who steals university parking permits from other students' cars, and the student who, under the pressure of a final examination, peeks at her neighbor's paper. And sometimes the misbehavior is downright dangerous or even criminal: the student in a residence hall who reaches out his window to cut a window-washer's rope just to see what will happen, the student who deviously forges a series of documents to give himself course credit for two full years of foreign-language classes, or the student who breaks into the university computer to increase her financial aid package. Staff members who work with the disturbing student know full well the range of their misdirected cleverness and creativity. The case illustrations included here are real, but details that might identify the students involved have been changed.

The purpose of this chapter is to describe ways in which the judicial process, in the context of a larger system such as the AISP model, can respond to the disturbing student in a manner that is constructive for the student as well as for the institution. To accomplish this end, the design of the judicial process must take into consideration its essential functions in the university community.

The judicial process has too often been seen as *either* regulatory *or* developmental. This has sometimes been reflected in the stereotypes of college deans and counselors that students, administrators, and faculty members hold. Remember Dean Wormer, of *Animal House* fame? It would be fair to say that his sole interest was regulating the behavior of his rather raucous students. At the other extreme, counselors have often been associated with June Cleaver's famous line, "Now, Ward, don't be too *hard* on the boys"—never wanting to impose punishment on her healthy, mischievous, all-American boys. Again, the stereotype is comic, but these dichotomous images are also reflected in well-respected sources of guidance for student affairs professionals.

Miller and Prince, in their landmark 1976 book, *The Future of Student Affairs,* discuss the application of developmental theory in student services. They give examples of the student development approach to such diverse areas as residence-hall programming, instruction and instructional support, counseling, and environmental management. These programs are seen as contributing to an educational environment in which students have access to the basic physical, monetary, and informational resources necessary for development; are free to risk disclosure of innermost thoughts and feelings without fear of attack or rejection; and are encouraged to interact with others freely. Moral development is mentioned as one of many developmental domains important for students, but the authors seem to think all of this will happen rather miraculously in the utopian context of a "truly developmental milieu" (p. 17). Miller and Prince do not even discuss the possible misconduct of students or the discipline process, but undoubtedly their suggestions would emphasize a therapy-oriented approach to the disturbing student. They represent the developmental pole of the regulatory-developmental dichotomy.

CAS Standards and Guidelines for Student Services/Development Programs, which is promulgated by the Council for the Advancement of Standards (1986), however, represents the almost purely regulatory approach. The council defines the mission of judicial programs and services almost solely in terms of the development and enforcement of rules. Rules must be "developed, disseminated, interpreted, and enforced." Students have legal rights, but the institution must "deal with student behavior problems in an effective manner" (p. 57). And the only mention of student development is in terms of "providing learning experiences for students who participate in the operation of the judicial system" (p. 57)—not for the students who may be guilty of misconduct.

Whereas student services professionals representing the regulatory approach have emphasized the interests of the institution rather than the interests of the student, student services professionals representing the developmental approach have emphasized the interests of the individual student. But an effective system for dealing with the disturbing student must balance *both* the interests of the individual student and the institution.

Functions of the Judicial Process

There are three distinct functions within the judicial process. These are the learning experience students have when they are involved in that process, the way in which the process upholds community standards for behavior, and the ways in which a student's involvement in the process can result in positive developmental outcomes. All of these functions must be acknowledged and incorporated into the design of the judicial process in order to maintain the balance between institutional and individual interests.

The Learning Experience. What do accused students learn from their experiences in the judicial process? *Case example:* Mary Beth was a sophomore pre-med major and most likely a type A disturbing student. She was referred to the judicial system because her chemistry professor believed she copied answers from another student's paper during a test.

She had no previous history of disciplinary infractions. To Mary Beth's surprise, she learned that there were two forms of the test—and she had copied the correct answers to the *other* test. This was the evidence with which she was initially confronted. What did she need to learn to be an effective participant in the discipline process? First, she needed to understand her rights as an accused student and understand how the discipline process on her campus worked. Without this knowledge, she could not be expected to represent herself well or to seek other representation. She needed to learn that there were choices to consider before she made decisions about how to handle her case, and she had to weigh both the short-term and the long-term implications of her decisions. She needed to learn that by remaining calm and utilizing her communication skills she could tell her side of the story most logically and persuasively. She needed to learn to manage the stress that inevitably accompanies being accused of wrongdoing so that any unnecessary disruption of her life could be minimized and she would be able to cope with both the discipline process and the consequences of her actions.

An effective judicial system draws the accused student into the discipline process as an active participant and teaches the skills necessary to manage that role effectively. This teaching process should not be haphazard or accidental. For fairness's sake, students must enter the process with their eyes open. Most students have a general understanding, for example, of their constitutional rights and the rights of persons accused in the criminal courts, but when they are accused of misconduct, they must quickly learn how these rights apply to them in the context of a university disciplinary process, where their rights are likely to be defined differently. Regardless of their guilt or innocence and the outcome of their case, working through the judicial process as an accused student should be an active learning experience in applied civics, decision making, communication skills, and stress management.

Maintaining a Viable Community. In order for education to take place, universities must maintain a reasonable level of order and a maximal level of integrity. A university is not an anonymous "it" that establishes rules for its own benefit. Every college and university is a community of students, faculty members, and staff members, and as a community it must establish guidelines for appropriate behavior in that setting. In any community, people should be safe from danger and affront, the security of personal property should be assured, and so forth. Yet because of the unique nature of a university community, integrity is a particularly important value, and rules that protect the integrity of the academic enterprise must also be established and enforced.

For years, university officials were considered to stand *in loco parentis* in their authority to make and enforce rules that would govern the academic community. As Ardaiolo (1983, p. 14) points out, institutions had the power to make "any rule concerning the moral, physical, and intellectual betterment of students that parents would make." In a number of pivotal decisions in the 1960s, however, the U.S. Supreme Court ruled that students must retain their constitutional rights of free speech, due process, and so forth, and this decision somewhat limited the scope of university authority. Nevertheless, the courts have defended the right of universities to make reasonable rules to maintain order and facilitate the teaching-learning process (for example, see *General Order of Judicial Standards of Procedures and Substance in Review of Student Discipline in Tax-Supported Institutions of Higher Education*, 1968). Reasonable people within the university community may disagree about which procedures and standards of behavior are appropriate, but there is no need for student services professionals to be apologetic about their role in enforcing those standards.

The Developmental Dimension. Can a student's experience of being accused of wrongdoing and working through the judicial system—regardless of whether the student is guilty or innocent, punished or not—result in a positive developmental outcome? Sometimes a student's experience in the judicial system creates a "teachable moment," or at the very least allows a staff member to assess the student's level of moral development.

Evans (1987) points out that student affairs professionals are obliged to attend to the moral and ethical dimensions of students' learning experiences, in accord with the mission statements of most colleges and universities. Moral development is, however, an inexact science. Student services professionals who work with discipline can only study what is known about the process of moral development and use their teaching and counseling skills to assist a particular student at a particular point in his or her development.

Case example: Victor was a first-semester freshman who realized immediately that there was a serious shortage of available parking spaces on campus. One day he looked down from his residence-hall window and noticed that the university police department had blocked off several spaces in preparation for repainting stripes on the pavement. The spaces were blocked with movable signs that said, "No Parking by Order of University Police." It occurred to Victor that this was the solution to his parking problem. After all, he had frequently been late to his afternoon classes when he returned from his off-campus job. When he left for work that day, he simply placed one of the signs in the trunk of his car, and the next day when he left for work, he put the sign in "his" space. The campus police, however, caught on to his solution, and several days later they were waiting for him when he returned to park. Referred to the judicial system, Victor admitted his wrongdoing and was willing to accept whatever penalty seemed reasonable. When asked by the student services professional handling his case why he thought his behavior was a problem, Victor was able to articulate an understanding of the moral implications of his actions. He had misappropriated the sign, and other students were denied access to parking because of the unfair advantage he gained by use of the sign. Victor was placed on disciplinary probation and encouraged to use his insight to make better decisions in the future. To the staff member it seemed that Victor was functioning at an age-appropriate level of moral development but had simply made a mistake. He was given a warning and given notice that any future, similar behavior would result in more severe consequences. Victor apparently learned his lesson, because he never again ran afoul of the system.

Case example: Samuel and Frank were seniors in engineering who shared a room at their fraternity house. Just before Halloween they came up with what seemed to them a great idea. They figured out an ingenious way of rigging a mannequin so that as cars passed in front of the house that evening, the mannequin would appear to dart into traffic. Their preparations for this prank were elaborate. They expected that the reactions of drivers would be hilarious! Unfortunately, the drivers did not share their sense of humor. The third passing car hit the dummy, and the driver believed he had killed someone. He was relieved but angry when he discovered the truth. The next morning he telephoned university officials to complain. When the student services professional assigned to their case sat down with Samuel and Frank to discuss their misconduct, they were incredulous that they had even been called in to discuss the situation. "What is the big deal? It was just a prank" said Frank. As the staff member pursued the discussion, the students were unable to see any problem with their behavior, other than the fact that they got caught. They were unable to comprehend the negative impact that their actions had had on other people and the safety hazard they had created.

Case example: Christine was a data processing major who had eight different assignments due the same week. One of them was a computer program that she just did not have time to finish. She persuaded a friend in the class to let her copy his program and submit it as her own. After all, they were both good students, and she would likely have come up with a similar program if she had had the time. Her instructor, however, realized that the two programs were too similar to be the independent work of two people and referred both students to the judicial system. Christine explained to the staff member that she had had too much to do that week and that she could have written the program herself, but she had just been too busy. She seemed confident that the staff member would understand her predicament and that her explanation would excuse her of any wrongdoing. Christine was most likely a type B disturbing student. She was manipulative and charming, and did not believe that she should be punished for any misbehavior. The staff member decided to evaluate Christine by discussing with her a series of hypothetical situations:

Counselor: Christine, how would you handle this situation? Let's say that once when you were in the teaching assistant's office you had had the chance to change one of your grades in her grade book. You wouldn't get caught. Would you do it?

Christine: Well, uh, maybe . . . if I hadn't done as well on the assignment as I could have . . .

CO: Okay. What if you had access to a computer terminal that would allow you to just go ahead and give yourself an "A" in this course. No one would ever know. Would you do it?

CH: Uh . . .

CO: Okay. Well, what if you could use that same computer terminal to raise your overall grade point average? No one would ever detect it. Would you do it?

CH: Well, it's possible . . .

CO: Okay. Let's say you could use that same terminal to just give yourself a degree. You wouldn't get caught. Would you do it?

CH: Oh, no. My parents wouldn't like that.

The intention of the staff member was to find the point at which Christine would say no and to help her examine her reasons. For Christine, it was not easy to see the ethical dimension of her decision-making process. As a result of her dishonest behavior, she received an "F" in the course, was placed on disciplinary probation, and contracted to return once a month for a year to continue the discussion with the staff member about how she handled the everyday ethical decisions in her life. These ongoing discussions also gave the student services professional working with her the opportunity to discuss her progress in school, her aspirations, and her relationships with friends and family.

The type A disturbing student is more likely to acknowledge his or her misbehavior and willingly accept the consequences, whereas the type B student is more likely to try to "con" his or her way out of difficulties. As a result, the type A/type B distinction is an important consideration for the student services professional in choosing a course of action that will have positive developmental outcomes.

Components of the Process

The details of judicial systems vary from campus to campus. Factors that determine the form of a judicial system include the size of the enrollment, the proportion of students who live on campus, whether the institution is public or private, and the tolerance level of the campus culture regarding certain kinds of disturbing behaviors. Nevertheless, the eight key components of the judicial process are the same. They include the identification and referral of alleged offenders, the assurance of due process, the assurance of confidentiality, the investigation of allegations, the interaction between staff members and students, the determination of guilt or innocence, decisions on penalties, and the attempt to approach the problem of campus misbehavior proactively.

Identification and Referral. Undoubtedly, some disturbing students succeed in concealing their misbehavior and never come to anyone's attention. However, most disturbing students usually call attention to themselves in some way. Whether students plagiarize an article or create a scene and are jailed for public intoxication, their chances of getting caught are probably greater than they imagine. In some way they have inadvertently caused their misbehavior to come to the attention of a faculty member, staff member, or campus security officer. Therefore, the extent to which faculty, staff, and campus security understand and feel supportive of the judicial process has a significant impact on the effectiveness of the system. A faculty member who thinks that every student accused of academic dishonesty is summarily expelled may be unlikely to make a referral. A head resident who believes that there are never any real consequences for misbehavior in the halls may be tempted to look the other way. And a security officer who does not understand what types of misbehavior are appropriate for referral may err in referring either every offense encountered or none of them.

Although they may not find the details of the judicial system inherently interesting, the faculty, staff, and campus security officers need to be well-informed about the judicial process. They need to understand the kinds of offenses that are covered under campus rules. They need to understand that students have certain rights, which must be protected at every stage of the discipline process. They need to understand that sometimes the wheels of the process seem to turn slowly because of the necessity of protecting these rights. And they need to have confidence that sanctions will actually be imposed when misbehavior is proven. If student services professionals take the initiative to disseminate essential information, many problems can be averted.

Educational efforts regarding the judicial system can take the form of articles in the student newspaper, presentations at departmental meetings, training sessions with police or security officers, brochures or fliers aimed at student services staff outside the judicial system, and all the other forms of communication that student services professionals are so expert at developing. The essential first step is to resolve that these efforts at communication are sufficiently important to invest the time and energy. However, lack of information or misinformation may not be the only causes of problems in the referral system.

Because individual faculty members discover incidents of misconduct less frequently than campus security officers or other university staff members, faculty members may experience some real turmoil in having to make a discipline referral. They may fear that their actions will ruin someone's life, or at the other extreme, they may be so angry with offending students that they want to banish them from their classrooms even before guilt or innocence has been established. Many faculty members feel personally violated when one of their students commits an act of scholastic dishonesty, and they may experience the full range of feelings that are associated with other forms of victimization, such as rape and assault. If student services staff members can address these feelings directly and empathically, they can ease the discomfort that faculty members may experience in making the referral.

Ensuring Due Process. In *Dixon* v. *Alabama State Board of Education* (1961), the Supreme Court defined the two basic elements of due process applicable in student disciplinary matters. Students must be notified of the charges, and they must be afforded a fair and impartial hearing with the opportunity to speak on their own behalf. Otherwise, the courts have tended to evaluate the adequacy of due process on a case-by-case basis, as Rhode and Math (1988) point out. This is both a blessing and a curse to student services administrators, since it means that the adequacy of a system can only be proven by going to court, and no one wants to be sued. Despite these ambiguities, judicial procedures must be tailored to meet the needs of the particular campus setting, and the courts have been receptive to this notion. Kaplin (1978, p. 239), however, has noted that "for the internal guidance of an administrator responsible for disciplinary procedures, the *Esteban* [from *Esteban* v. *Central Missouri State College* (1969)] requirements provide a very useful checklist." Specifically, the *Esteban* decision required that the accused student receive written notice of the charges at least ten days in advance of a hearing; that the hearing be held before a person having the power to impose penalties; that there be an opportunity for the accused student to review evidence in advance of the hearing; that a student be allowed to bring legal counsel to furnish advice, but not necessarily to represent them; that the accused student have the opportunity to present his or her side of the story, in writing, orally, and by the testimony of witnesses; that the accused student have the opportunity to hear all adverse evidence and to question adverse witnesses; that the decision in the case be made solely on the basis of the evidence; that the student be furnished with a written statement of the findings of fact; and that the student be afforded the option to make a recording of the hearing at his or her own expense. Aside from these specific guidelines laid out by the federal appeals court in the *Esteban* case, the courts have simply evaluated disciplinary decisions on the basis of the fundamental fairness of procedures.

Ensuring Confidentiality. The confidentiality of the judicial process is crucial for both legal and developmental reasons. The Family Educational Rights and Privacy Act, commonly referred to as the Buckley

Amendment, of course, protects the privacy of educational records, including disciplinary records. Students who are over eighteen years of age are given control over their own records, and in general it is only with their written permission that others can be informed of disciplinary action.

In terms of the student's personal development, these privacy provisions have both positive and negative consequences. On the positive side, the restrictions remind students that they are indeed regarded as autonomous individuals and reinforce for them the personal responsibility they bear for their actions and the decisions they make in the discipline process. Most students find it reassuring that they can control access to knowledge about their disciplinary difficulties. However, some students find it difficult to tell *anyone* about their situation and may as a result become withdrawn and isolated at a time when they especially need the support of family and close friends. Because of the manipulative pattern of type B disturbing students, they may be more likely to run a "con" on friends and family and may even claim that they are attending classes when they have in fact been suspended or expelled. Type A students, in contrast, may simply feel overwhelmed by having become involved in the discipline process, and as a result they may hide their difficulties from the people whose support they need the most. In these situations, student services professionals may find the Buckley restrictions frustrating because they are unable to directly contact these students' natural support systems. And parents find the Buckley restrictions particularly frustrating when they have some idea that their son or daughter is having problems but they cannot get information directly from administrators without their son's or daughter's permission.

The overall developmental impact of the Buckley restrictions is positive, however, in that it reinforces a student's sense of personal control and responsibility. For those students whose natural reaction may be to withdraw, the student services professional may assist by asking the student to make a promise to tell someone about his or her plight and allowing the student to rehearse that conversation. Telling *someone* will help the student avoid the trap of personal isolation.

Another frustration for student services professionals is the fact that the Buckley Amendment restricts details of discipline cases from being communicated to the campus community at large. This seriously limits the deterrent effect that such information might have, since the effect of "sanitized" stories (with all identifying detail removed) is just not as helpful.

Getting the Facts. Working in a student affairs office is actually very similar to being a detective. First, working in the judicial system requires healthy levels of both curiosity and skepticism. As the story of a disciplinary infraction unfolds, it is essential that the staff member gather and record as much detailed information as possible, even when it may at first seem trivial or unimportant. This applies to conversations with accused students, witnesses, and any faculty or staff members involved. And not all information can be taken at face value. People sometimes lie—as difficult as that may be to accept for the student services professional who wants to believe in the basic honesty of people. At the same time, pursuing every lead and maintaining a healthy skepticism does not mean that the investigating staff member is "out to get" the student, but rather that only the most thorough and careful investigation will yield helpful results for all parties involved. Most likely, the staff member would just as soon discover that no wrongdoing has occurred.

The Interpersonal Process. Though all eight of the components of the judicial process listed here are important, the quality of the interaction between a student and a staff member has perhaps the greatest potential impact on the developmental outcomes of the process. Faced with a student who may be experiencing tremendous stress, most student services professionals naturally lead with warmth and supportive counseling skills. But there is a difference in this setting. Empathy and support must be balanced with confrontation.

For some professionals, it is tempting to make the consequences light for students who seem sufficiently repentant. This may be particularly true for the type A student, who may appear isolated, immature, and particularly in need of help. But acting on this impulse is likely to short-circuit the discipline process and ultimately be a disservice to students who may get the impression that they are not accountable for their actions. The staff member can pursue the case tenaciously while still conveying concern and respect for the student as a person by keeping in mind the distinction between who the student *is* and what misdeeds he or she may have committed. Nevertheless, students need to know that whether guilty or innocent, their case has been thoroughly and carefully considered.

Of course, not all students immediately appear remorseful or distressed. The type B student, particularly, may attempt to charm his or her way out of the problem or may become uncooperative or even belligerent. These students, too, need to understand that they are accountable for their actions. They may, however, require a more direct and assertive response from staff members, who can still convey a fundamental sense of respect and concern.

A staff member may discover that some or both of these types of students in fact need to be referred to the campus mental health system to deal with the situations they are facing. They may not have initially been categorized as disturbed/disturbing but would still benefit from working with a therapist. For example, a referral may be indicated for a student who seems unable to muster the energy to take an active part in resolving the case and who may be clinically depressed. Or a referral may be indicated for the student who "attaches" himself or herself to the staff member and makes weekly or daily visits to the office even after the case is resolved. For these and other types of students, therapy is beneficial.

Determining Guilt or Innocence. In the court's view of the judicial process, the guilt or innocence of a student is determined in the hearing. Hearings must be held before impartial decision makers, must afford the accused student an opportunity to tell his or her side of the story, must allow for legal counsel to be present (but not necessarily to represent the student), and must result in a decision made solely on the basis of evidence presented.

In practice, the disciplinary "hearing" can take many forms, depending on the unique characteristics of a particular campus environment. Evidence may be presented before a judicial board composed of students, faculty members, administrators, or any combination of these, or before an individual hearing officer, who would most likely be an administrator, faculty member, or (in some systems) an attorney or other person from outside the campus community. On some campuses, students may choose whether to have their case heard before the judicial board or before a single hearing officer. And on many campuses, students have the option of waiving their right to a hearing altogether, choosing intead to make the equivalent of a *nolo contendere* plea in criminal court—accepting a penalty without admitting guilt per se. All of these alternatives can be formulated in such a way that they meet the requirements prescribed by the courts.

One aspect of the hearing process that is often difficult to understand for students and student services professionals alike is the standard of proof required to render a finding of guilty. The standard of proof required in administrative procedures (such as student discipline) is defined as the greater weight of the credible evidence. In contrast, the standard of proof required in criminal matters is defined as beyond a reasonable doubt, and in civil matters it is the preponderance of the evidence. If academic dishonesty were a criminal offense, the judicial procedures would be altogether different. In order to find Mary Beth guilty, for instance, the case against her would have to include a witness who had actually seen her looking at and copying from the other student's test paper. Otherwise, she might claim that she simply arrived at her answers by guessing, and it would be theoretically possible for her to have gotten the answers in that way, thus making the evidence of her answers merely circumstantial at best. As it is in the university discipline process, the unlikelihood of Mary Beth's simply having guessed a whole set of correct answers for another form of the test makes it possible to conclude "by the greater weight of the credible evidence " that she cheated.

Deciding Penalties. When a student accused of wrongdoing is found guilty, either by his or her own admission or through a hearing, the decision as to the appropriate penalty has to be made. Sometimes the student services professional is authorized to actually make the decision, and sometimes the decision takes the form of a recommendation to a judicial board or hearing officer.

Acknowledging the broad educational mission of colleges and universities, the courts have provided sufficient latitude so that institutional rules usually permit the university to tailor the penalty to a particular student's situation. The quandary that most often arises for the student services professional is whether to take a more rehabilitative or a more punitive approach. A good penalty, however, encompasses both approaches. It confronts the student with the consequences of his or her actions, and it challenges the student to reassess past decisions and learn new behaviors for the future. The case of Christine illustrates this point. Most people would not view the "F" she received in the course as particularly rehabilitative—certainly Christine did not—but failing the course is the logical consequence of submitting another student's work as her own. She does not deserve any credit for the course. Even if she had in fact done all of the other course work herself, that work must now be viewed as suspect. The "F" in the course also forces her to realize that academic dishonesty is unacceptable in a university community. At the same time, failing the course in itself is not likely to help Christine reevaluate her decision and change her behavior in the future. For that reason, the student services professional involved chose to have her return periodically to continue their discussion. This contract was made as a stipulation in the terms of her probation, so that if she failed to keep her commitment, additional consequences would follow.

Depending on the circumstances and the nature of a student's misbehavior, a wide range of possible penalties is available to the student services professional. If an offense involves damage, an appropriate penalty likely includes restitution. If an offense involves some less tangible harm to the university community, a period of community services might provide a form of symbolic restitution, and depending on the service placement, it might expose the student to models of more appropriate behavior. If an offense involves drugs or alcohol, a referral to the campus substance abuse educator is called for. And if a student needs the opportunity to reflect on his or her values or to learn a new decision-making process, an individually designed educational task or assignment may be in order. Though a wide range of options is available, penalties must reflect the norms of the local campus community and be sufficiently consistent to be perceived as fair. On one campus the automatic penalty for any academic dishonesty might be suspension, whereas on another campus there might be a range of penalties, depending on the degree of premeditation involved. Each of these approaches could be "right" for that campus. Similarly, two students on the same campus who copy from other students' papers might be given the same academic penalty but receive different rehabilitative sanctions.

Taking a Proactive Approach. Of all the areas of student services, the judicial system is perhaps the hardest to approach proactively—not because it is difficult to form ideas for proactive efforts, but because by its very nature the process is so reactive. Every time the phone rings, it signals a problem. And the phone rings so often that all of the staff member's time is devoted to dealing with students who have already caused problems. By taking a proactive approach, however, at least some students can be steered away from the various forms of misbehavior that would bring them into the judicial system.

Proactive measures can inform students of what behavior is proscribed, what rights accused students have, and what a typical sanction would be for various offenses. Information can be disseminated via brochures, videotapes, newspaper articles, workshops, panel discussions, and so forth. Getting students involved in this effort can offer the dual benefits of enhancing the credibility of the information presented and capitalizing on the pressure that students can exert on their peers to encourage positive behavior.

Importance of the Team Approach

In the initial chapter of this volume, Delworth describes the campus intervention team as a model for developing and implementing assessment and intervention programs for disturbed, disturbing, and disturbed/disturbing students. Although the format she proposes tends toward the idealistic, the model stresses the importance of creating and maintaining a close working relationship among key staff members. This teamwork is crucial for the effective functioning of the judicial system.

The form that the team concept takes may vary from campus to campus, but the essential ingredients are the same. First, key staff members must know each other well enough to communicate easily—brainstorming alternatives, developing strategies, pointing out problems, refining solutions, and so forth. Judicial services staff members and campus security officers, for example, need to feel free to call on counselors when trying to understand the complexities of a student's behavior. In situations such as these, the expertise of counseling staff members can be invaluable. Second, they need to have confidence in each other's judgments about the gravity of a problem situation. They should be secure in the knowledge that phone calls will be returned and that when a colleague asks to interrupt a meeting, the situation warrants it. Third, they need to understand the constraints under which their colleagues work. For example, it is incumbent on the student services administrator to understand that a student's conversations with a counselor are strictly confidential, and counselors must understand the rules and procedures that govern the discipline process. It is important for counselors and student services administrators to recognize that in some situations it may be necessary for campus security officers to take immediate action to remove a student from campus without the benefit of consultation, and police officers must understand the due-process rights afforded students in the judicial system. Finally, the campus intervention team needs to share a strong sense of commitment to serving the best interests of the students while protecting and maintaining a viable campus community. Sharing the same commitments provides a firm foundation for the team members' working together to solve problems.

Conclusion

Students referred to the judicial system are often on the edge—the edge of the community, in that they have violated the community's norms—and yet at the same time they are potentially on the cutting edge of their own personal development. A successful intervention on the part of the judicial system confronts students with the consequences of their actions while furthering the maturity of their developmental process.

References

Ardaiolo, F. P. "What Process Is Due?" In M. J. Barr (ed.), *Student Affairs and the Law.* New Directions for Student Services, no. 22. San Francisco: Jossey-Bass, 1983.

Council for the Advancement of Standards. *CAS Standards and Guidelines for Student Services/Development Programs.* Iowa City, Iowa: American College Testing Program, 1986.

Dixon v. Alabama State Board of Education, 294 F.2d 150 (5th Cir. 1961), *cert. denied* 368 U.S. 930, 82 S. Ct. 368 (1961).

Esteban v. Central Missouri State College, 277 F. Supp. 649 (W.D. Mo. 1967), *affirmed* 415 F.2d 1077 (8th Cir. 1969).

Evans, N. J. "A Framework for Assisting Student Affairs Staff in Fostering Moral Development." *Journal of Counseling and Development,* 1987, *66* (4), 191–194.

General Order of Judicial Standards of Procedures and Substance in Review of Student Discipline in Tax-Supported Institutions of Higher Education, 45 F.R.D. 133 (W.D. Mo. 1968).

Kaplin, W. A. *The Law of Higher Education: Legal Implications of Administrative Decision Making.* San Francisco: Jossey-Bass, 1978.

Miller, T. K., and Prince, J. S. *The Future of Student Affairs: A Guide to Student Development for Tomorrow's Higher Education.* San Francisco: Jossey-Bass, 1976.

Rhode, S. R., and Math, M. G. "Student Conduct, Discipline, and Control: Understanding Institutional Options and Limits." In M. J. Barr (ed.), *Student Services and the Law: A Handbook for Practitioners.* San Francisco: Jossey-Bass, 1988.

John D. Ragle is assistant to the dean of students at the University of Texas at Austin. He served previously as assistant dean for Student Judicial Services and is currently pursuing a doctoral degree in counseling psychology.

Sharon H. Justice is dean of students at the University of Texas at Austin. She is responsible for freshman services, emphasis programs, retention services, campus activities, and the administration of the judicial system.

*Colleges and universities must provide a safety net and
a coordinated set of services for psychologically disturbed
students.*

The Disturbed
College Student

Donna L. McKinley, Daniel S. Dworkin

Epidemiological studies using various samples report similar results:
approximately 20 percent of the adult population of the United States
evinces sufficient psychological disturbance to require treatment (Freedman, 1984). A recent study of college-bound high school students and
inner-city high school students in Chicago reported similar results for
both populations (Offer and Spiro, 1987). Given these results, it seems
fair to assume that 10 to 20 percent of enrolled college students experience enough emotional distress to warrant some type of psychological
treatment.

Student affairs staff members usually have responsibility to do something about or with the student who is showing signs of disturbance.
Responsible staff members range from the frontline residence-hall or activities staff member, who must deal with the student on a daily basis, to the
chief student personnel officer, who has responsibility for setting university policy on dealing with disturbed students and for allocating resources
for services. The purpose of this chapter is first to provide information
about psychological disturbances found in students and how they come
about and then to make suggestions regarding a comprehensive service
delivery system to meet the needs of the students and the institution. We
first describe four broad categories of psychological disturbance among

U. Delworth (ed.). *Dealing with the Behavioral and Psychological Problems of Students.*
New Directions for Student Services, no. 45. San Francisco: Jossey-Bass, Spring 1989.

students. Then we consider the elements of a comprehensive campus response. Finally, we address the need for coordination of responses.

Categories of Disturbed Students

Delworth in Chapter One defines the disturbed student as one who "exhibits specific behaviors and patterns of behavior that are out of sync with other students and are often marked by a moving away from or setting themselves against others." There is a pattern of isolation from others as well as self-rejecting behavior. The disturbed student's capacity for healthy emotional, cognitive, and social functioning is severely impaired. The student's development in any or all of these areas is not proceeding normally because the student cannot cope with the pressures of student life. As described in Delworth's Assessment-Intervention of Student Problems (AISP) model, the problem may be chronic or situational. There may be specific, observable events that precede the onset of disturbed behavior, or the change may arise without warning. Students may come to campus presenting symptoms of disturbance, or the problems may develop after they arrive.

The possible manifestations of disturbance vary widely. Some students simply do not look very happy, or perhaps they treat everything as a joke or as an excuse to make a hostile remark or gesture. Grades drop or suddenly improve, but the student avoids previously pleasurable activities. Alcohol or drug use may increase; listlessness, sleeplessness, weight loss or gain, withdrawal from activities or friends may be symptoms; an eating disorder may develop. In more extreme forms, the student may report hearing voices or smelling strange odors, initiate a variety of frequently repeated rituals, withdraw into a rigid fetal position, attempt suicide, or take on an entirely new personality.

Determining the exact nature and cause of a psychological disturbance is the province of the campus mental health professionals, but until a referral can be made, other student affairs staff members need to know how they can help. The following descriptions of various psychological disturbances are intended to contribute to an understanding how students become disturbed, what assessment information is available to the student affairs staff, and some interventions that may be appropriate.

We have identified four broad categories of disturbed students. For the most part, examples refer to traditional-age undergraduate students; however, manifestations of disturbance in older students are discussed when appropriate.

Situational. The most common disturbances are situational or stress related. These fall into the category disturbed student type A-B 1 in the AISP model. No matter how worldly or experienced, the entering student is confronted with a new environment, which has new demands, new people, and a new set of social and academic rules. Depending on how much the new environment resembles past environments, this adjustment may go very smoothly. But it may result in periods of dysfunction for some students. The symptoms may be quite severe and lead to very serious consequences, even death, if not addressed, but the causes are fairly common occurrences and are readily understood. Minority students moving from an ethnic neighborhood into a predominantly white institution must be considered a population at particular risk. Extreme withdrawal, depression, and substance abuse are common reactions.

Peer staff members in residence halls and other student services programs can play a very important role in identifying students experiencing this type of adjustment problem and in helping students resolve the difficulty. The manifestation may be of either type A or type B. In either case a peer counselor who has already made the effort to get acquainted with the student is in a good position to approach the student with an inquiry into how the student feels about campus life. Letting the student know that many others, including the peer counselor if appropriate, experience difficulty in fitting into campus life is both supportive and a good assessment tool. If the student is not responsive after repeated attempts over a period of a week or less, then the peer staff members should consult with supervisors. Obviously, in the case of extreme withdrawal or aggressive behavior, consultation should occur immediately.

For any student such events as the death of a family member or friend; loss of an important relationship; a natural disaster in the home community; roommate, marital, or family conflicts; academic difficulties; or a serious injury or illness may be sufficiently stressful to cause the student to manifest symptoms of psychological disturbance. Peer staff members can be quite helpful in this circumstance as well by offering support, sharing information about their experiences in similar situations, helping with arrangements for leaves of absence from campus, and making referrals if the student feels the need for more extensive exploration of feelings and reactions.

Developmental. A second category of psychological disturbances among students may be referred to as normal developmental crises. The AISP category for disturbed student A-B 2 describes this student. For traditional-age college students, the college years tend to coincide with a number of important developments in the transition from adolescence to adulthood. A great deal of the psychological energy of students is expended on such questions as What do I want to do with my life? What kind of relationships do I want to have and how do I form them? What are my values and how do I implement them? What talents do I have and what doors does a realistic appraisal of my talents open or close? Not having answers is a significant source of turmoil and stress. Often the emerging answers conflict with parental expectations, previous dreams or commitments, or self-evaluations. Many older students are returning to these important questions as they return to college or enter for the first time. In addition they may be struggling with issues of self-confidence, being a single parent, living in an environment dominated by younger students, and trying to integrate their new role of student with their more familiar adult self-image.

Though the process of answering these questions is a positive challenge and a necessary part of life, the stress on a student may be quite severe and can lead to dysfunctional behavior until the crisis is resolved or the student can be engaged in the process in a positive manner. Many student affairs staff members have a background in student development theory and can help students understand their struggle with these issues. Faculty members as well as student affairs staff members can be most helpful when they are willing to disclose their own struggles and processes of developing personal answers to important universal questions. For many students in the throes of an important developmental crisis, all they need is reassurance that what they are experiencing is normal.

Family of Origin Issues. Many students come to college with unresolved conflicts and difficult personal histories. These students constitute the third category of disturbance. In the AISP model they may be categorized as disturbed student type A-B 3; type A-B 4 is even more likely. Ideal families who respond to all the challenges of living and child rearing in a psychologically healthy manner are rare, in spite of the expectations developed from story books, television, and the popular psychological literature. Most families have conflicts and residual scars that individual members must resolve for themselves. Some families develop extremely dysfunctional means of dealing with issues, and the college-bound offspring of these families bring a great deal of excess psychological baggage to college. Psychological and physical abuse, incest, alcoholism, criminal activities, and psychosis are found in all strata of society and have taken their toll on persons who find their way to college. Students who have survived dysfunctional families and succeeded in getting to college have developed certain coping skills, but often these are very rigid. In the new environment these coping skills may no longer work. For example, the psychological numbing characteristic of many victims of abuse interferes with the forming of the close relationships often expected in college living situations, student organizations, and athletic teams.

Depending on which stage of the student's development the dysfunctional family system had most impact, the disturbance may be quite profound. Many adult children of an alcoholic parent grew up in very chaotic and unpredictable environments, where their normal needs were not met consistently, and so they have great difficulty with relationships, trust, control, and intimacy. Those students who feel that they have never been able to please their parents may experience a crisis under the stress of trying to satisfy all academic and social demands, or they may rebel and simply disregard all community expectations. In any case, students bring problems to college as a result of their interaction with unhealthy home environments, which did not provide adequate nurturance and opportunity to develop effective psychological coping skills.

The academic environment also contributes to a breakdown of the coping mechanisms used to survive in dysfunctional families by encouraging free exploration of ideas, values, and social structures. Student development and family and health education programs expose these students to more ideal forms of human interaction and encourage them to analyze their personal histories and reactions. Though in the long run this examination is useful for the student and for society, since the development of healthier coping skills will keep the student from perpetuating a dysfunctional family system, the immediate consequence is likely to be a strong manifestation of disturbance.

Biologically Based Disorders. The fourth category of disturbed students includes those experiencing a disease process. The most likely AISP category is disturbed student type A-B 5. These students are victims of specific psychiatric disorders to which they have been genetically predisposed and which are most likely to emerge in late adolescence or early adulthood. The students in this category have an organic dysfunction for which medical treatment is possible. Some types of depression, manic behavior, suicidal behavior, impulsive anger, convulsions, memory loss, and psychosis have been shown to be biologically based. Behavior may take the form of complete withdrawal, for example, sitting in a fetal position on the floor and refusing to move, hearing voices, and experiencing intense paranoia, anger, or anxiety so that the student's behavior appears to be completely out of control.

Disturbed students whose symptoms are long-standing and either do not change or grow worse are highly likely to require assistance from mental health professionals. If the disturbed student's concerns are not resolved through the support and information provided by the student affairs staff member, consultation with and referral to a mental health professional is indicated.

Drug Involvement. In responding to the disturbed behavior of college students, specific mention must be made of drug and alcohol involvement. Many types of drugs are readily available on most college campuses, and experimentation with drugs is commonly associated with college attendance. Even minor experimentation with certain drugs or combinations of drugs can produce bizarre behavior and should be considered as a possible cause of any incident. Drugs, especially alcohol, are sometimes used by students trying to cope with anxiety. Most students who experiment with drugs and alcohol in college do not become abusers. But some, perhaps as many as 10 percent on a given campus, do develop serious drug-related problems. If chemical dependency plays a part in a student's problematic behavior, it must be identified and treated before any other interventions can be used. Residence-hall and student activities staff members are in a particularly good position to know whether a student is having difficulty with alcohol or drugs. Their training should include instruction in the identification, confrontation, and referral of drug-related behavior problems.

Environmental Contributors. In addition to the student's home environment, the environment of the university can soothe or aggravate a student's psychological disturbances. In some cases even the most positive aspects of a university contribute to opening old wounds, which may bring about an opportunity either to resolve the dysfunction or to be consumed by it. In other respects the university may contribute to the development of a disturbance either by omission or by commission. When a group of students are at risk—for example, the minority student population referred to earlier or students in obvious distress—and no support services are provided to assist them in making a healthy adjustment, then the institution has contributed to disturbance by omission. When administrators condone an environment that promotes alcohol abuse, tolerates sexual harassment, uses teaching methods based on intimidation, and promises opportunities that do not really exist, the contribution to the development of disturbance is direct.

Institutional Response

Some members of the academic community do not feel that it is the role of the institution to "take care" of students who are not functioning effectively within the campus environment. From their perspective any student who is evincing psychological disturbance should simply be removed from campus. But close scrutiny reveals that many disturbed students are holding their own academically. Often they are bright and can negotiate the academic system very well. Moreover, except in institutions with absolutely open-door admissions policies, all students admitted to the university, including those who appear disturbed, have demonstrated sufficient capacity to handle college work. Even if they are having academic difficulty currently, past performance portends well for the future if the distress can be alleviated. So it is not a simple matter of the institution's having let some historically dysfunctional persons slip through the admissions process. Emotional distress does not necessarily mean that a student cannot perform well in the classroom. The task for those responsible in the university is to take stock of the student's current level of functioning and to determine the best course of action for the student, the other members of the university community, and the university itself. This assignment most often falls to the student affairs professionals on campus.

Student Services Perspectives. In deciding which systems and services are needed for disturbed students on campus, the Banning and Kaiser (1974) categorization of perspectives on student services provides a helpful frame of reference. The "unenlightened" perspective is a rigid adherence to the philosophy that some students are unfit or unprepared for college and should be barred from admission or automatically removed when they display evidence of problems. The "adjustment," or remedial, perspective is built on the assumption that students who have problems can be assisted by counseling and other services to help them enjoy and make better use of the opportunities of the college environment. The "developmental" perspective acknowledges that there are personal and life skills that are needed in order to progress through the demands of college—for example, the ability to interact productively with others, the adoption of a flexible coping system, and the development of a healthy balance between work and recreation. Finally, the "ecological" perspective examines the interaction between students and the institutional environment.

Given the earlier descriptions of the causes of disturbance observed in college students, it follows that a comprehensive campus response should include the ecological, developmental, and adjustment perspectives. The campus counseling center or primary mental health service should incorporate all these perspectives in the design and implementation of mental health services. Though this agency is the focal point for organizing such services, it cannot do the job by itself. Counseling services must be integrated with living units, judicial systems, health services, academic units, student organizations, security forces, and other student support services.

Adjustment and Developmental Services. Adjustment counseling is the most traditional of the counseling and student personnel services. A student suffering from undue stress often finds a counselor who, in a few sessions of supportive and self-exploratory counseling, helps the student resolve a conflict; find appropriate outlets for social, academic, or spiritual needs; or develop some necessary coping skills. Assisting students in resolving normal developmental crises has a rich history in student personnel services. In addition to providing such services in a counseling context, there is the more complex task of offering developmental services within a preventive framework. Here the task becomes one of ascertaining which students need the service and enticing them to make use of it before problems develop. Sometimes such services can be delivered through curricular offerings so that academic credit becomes the enticement.

Many adjustment- and developmentally oriented services can be provided by faculty and staff members outside the formal mental health services system. For example, residence-hall staff members can lead discussion groups and workshops on typical concerns of college students. With a little assistance from counseling professionals through resource materials, consultation on workshop design, or stimulus films that can be seen on close-circuit or cable television networks, the university can offer programs that are quite sophisticated in content and reach many more students than can be reached by the counseling personnel directly. Faculty advisers can also provide developmentally oriented advising and career counseling. Student affairs professionals in minority student support programs also provide developmental and adjustment counseling services, which are often more favorably accepted from the student affairs office than from the counseling center. Through outreach programs, the counseling center can, in addition to its usual services, support other university services that provide assistance for students with adjustment or developmental concerns.

Removal of Students. The unenlightened perspective, which calls for immediate removal of a problem student, also has a place in the campus mental health system. Some disturbed students simply cannot be allowed to remain in the campus environment because their presence constitutes a danger to themselves or to others. Implementation of this perspective requires extreme caution and flexibility in order to avoid infringing on the student's civil and legal rights.

Several legal issues must be taken into consideration. Section 504 of the Rehabilitation Act of 1973 provides the same protection for the mentally ill that it does for persons with physical handicaps. Therefore, it must be clearly demonstrated that the student is unable to perform the work required. State laws apply as well. All states specify the circumstances under which a person may be hospitalized involuntarily. Often it is necessary to demonstrate that the person is a clear and present danger to self or others. If a student is to be removed from campus, the relevant state law provides the guidance and the requirements for removal. In a residence hall or campus situation there are contractual agreements and standards of conduct that provide the framework within which an action can be taken. Due-process requirements apply to this situation as they would in any disciplinary action that is going to affect the student's status in the institution. Pavela (1985) provides useful guidelines for dealing with the disturbed student when removal from campus is a consideration.

Protection of the student's right to be different must be balanced with institutional requirements to provide an environment that is safe and conducive to academic pursuits for all its inhabitants. A chronically suicidal student living in a residence hall is a familiar example of a situation in which the disturbed student creates negative consequences for a large number of people. Other students become preoccupied with the safety of the student, residence-hall staff members feel responsible, anxiety interferes with sleep and needed recreation, the counselor's personal life is disrupted, and nobody accomplishes very much academic work. In this situation it is most helpful to have a mental health professional work with the student while the residence-hall staff and the affected residents set up a plan of action that all can agree to. It is particularly important to agree on limits of responsibility of the staff and other residents and what action will be taken if the disturbed student requires more assistance than is appropriate for them to give.

An Ecological Approach. The ecological perspective is embodied in the question What is it about this environment that is causing or contributing to a student's distress? This leads to a series of questions: What are the characteristics of the student? What are the characteristics of the environment? What happened in the transaction between the student and the environment to produce disturbed behavior? Does something in the environment need to change? or something in the student?

For the student affairs or mental health professional, the implementation of an ecological perspective requires a change in traditional thinking. Most professional training focuses on understanding the individual; an ecological perspective requires that the camera be focused more broadly. Tools such as the Ecological Diagnostic Classification Plan (Hurst and McKinley, 1988) can be helpful. This perspective also requires some new strategies for compiling data on clients of a mental health service. Understanding individual psychopathology is not enough. Epidemiological strategies from the public health field can be useful in determining the common external agents that contribute to disturbance and that can in turn become the focus for changing the environment.

A Comprehensive Delivery System. In dealing with the disturbed student, the challenge on a campus is to provide a large enough safety net so that those students experiencing psychological disturbance can be offered effective and timely individual assistance and so that the environmental contributors can be identified and modified as well. Though the campus counseling center will probably be the focal point for the coordination and delivery of services, a comprehensive services delivery system requires careful coordination among the various campus units concerned about student welfare. Representatives of all involved units should meet on a regular basis for the purposes of clarifying responsibilities, coordinating responses, sharing resources, identifying and resolving problems, and agreeing on philosophy and procedures. Official appointment and sanction for this campus intervention team from the vice-president for student affairs or the equivalent can be helpful in garnering the resources needed to provide services and increasing the likelihood of receptivity when environmental changes are recommended.

Effective working relationships among units are essential to a comprehensive service delivery system. There should be communication between campus mental health professionals and all university or college staff members who will have contact with students, so that the entire campus can be the safety net. This should include academic faculty members, coaches, campus clergy, food service and maintenance personnel, and health professionals, as well as all the student development and activities staff members. Cooperation between the campus mental health system and law enforcement systems can facilitate comprehensive evaluation of emergency situations and can make psychological treatment available on a mandatory or voluntary basis. There should be collaboration between the campus mental health system and the student discipline system so that students with disturbances manifested in misbehavior are properly identified and referred for treatment.

There must be an especially effective working relationship between campus mental health professionals and staff members in the residence units. The close proximity of the living arrangements requires that the residence hall itself be considered when dealing with a disturbed student. For example, when a residence-hall student is treated in a medical facility for a suicide attempt, the follow-up planning should include the residence-hall staff and a roommate at least. Often a whole floor of a residence hall will have become involved in the situation, and careful debriefing can help those students get back to their studies and assist them in being a positive force in the student's recovery. The residence-hall staff members should insist that the mental health professional confer with them before the student returns from the hospital. They will have many concerns, including how to allay the fears of other students that the incident will recur, and what degree of responsibility residence-hall staff members should take in monitoring the disturbed student. In addition, they may be angry that the professional was not able to keep the student in the hospital, given the severity of the incident. General guidelines for this and other types of situations should be worked out by the campus intervention team. Even with such planning, decisions regarding response will be difficult and require flexibility. Without a comprehensive game plan, however, the danger increases that a crisis will turn into a tragedy.

The issue of confidentiality is important to address when developing a system for responding to disturbed students. A rigid interpretation of the confidential nature of counseling relationships would dictate that the mental health professional not release any information about a client without express written permission, except in certain circumstances dictated by state law. In some circumstances such an interpretation may not be in the student's best interest, and the ethical principle of primary commitment to the client's best interest should take precedence. Two examples will serve to illustrate the point.

Residence-hall staff members make frequent referrals to counseling professionals. Usually the student will give permission for the counselor to let the referring person know that treatment has been started as suggested. Occasionally, the student does not give permission, and this lack of information sharing contributes to that hall staff member's inadvertent interference in treatment. The residence-hall staff members can be alerted that they should have follow-up contact with the counselor. Within the context of a collaborative relationship, the counselor's response, "I don't have a release of information to discuss the student," can be correctly interpreted to mean that therapy has begun but that the counselor is not free to discuss it. Without preparation for dealing with confidentiality constraints faced by counseling professionals, the residence-hall staff can easily interpret the counselor's response as unwillingness to cooperate.

Another situation might involve a severely disturbed student whose voluntary or involuntary hospitalization cannot be accomplished. Even if the student does not wish to have parents notified, the mental health or student affairs professional may decide that the student's greater good would be served by getting the family involved. An important caution in this situation is to make every possible effort to find out enough about the family to be reasonably certain that the family will be a positive force in the treatment. Residence-hall staff, roommates, and a faculty adviser may all have relevant observations to contribute. The campus intervention team should develop guidelines to cover this situation, and these should include the circumstances under which such a decision would be considered and a list of persons who would need to be involved in the decision. At minimum a legal opinion and a mental health professional's evaluation should be required.

Additionally, a comprehensive service delivery system should include both mental health and student affairs professionals with skills to develop environmental change strategies and systematic student development programs. The mental health system needs psychologists with well-developed diagnostic skills in order to accurately differentiate adjustment and situational distresses from severe psychopathology and organic processes. Psychiatrists must also be available to provide medical diagnosis and intervention and assistance with hospitalization. Any student health insurance program should include mental health benefits so that referral can be made for specific treatments that are not available on campus.

Many observers have discussed the societal changes occurring along with our progression from a technology-based to an information-based society. One important aspect of these changes has been the increased concern for human resources and human potential. Many businesses and industries have responded by developing employee assistance and health programs. Colleges and universities can respond by providing adequate resources and opportunities for students to resolve their psychological crises and get on with the business of becoming productive, educated citizens. The benefits will accrue not only for the student but also for the institution and society.

References

Banning, J. H., and Kaiser, L. "An Ecological Perspective Model for Campus Design." *Personnel and Guidance Journal*, 1974, *32* (6), 370-375.

Freedman, D. X. "Psychiatric Epidomiology Counts." *Archives of General Psychiatry*, 1984, *41*, 931-933.

Hurst, J. C., and McKinley, D. L. "An Ecological Diagnostic Classification Plan." *Journal of Counseling and Development*, 1988, *66* (5), 228-232.

Offer, D., and Spiro, R. "The Disturbed Adolescent Goes to College." *Journal of American College Health*, 1987, *35* (5), 209-214.

Pavela, G. *The Dismissal of Students with Mental Disorders: Legal Issues, Policy Considerations, and Alternative Responses*. Asheville, N.C.: College Administration Publications, 1985.

Donna L. McKinley is an assistant vice-president for student affairs and an affiliate faculty member in the Department of Psychology at Colorado State University. She holds the Diplomate in Counseling from the American Board of Professional Psychology.

Daniel S. Dworkin is the coordinator of clinical services at the University Counseling Center and is assistant professor in the Department of Psychology at Colorado State University. His interests include mental health administration and the application of metaphysical principles to Western psychotherapy.

The disturbed/disturbing student exhibits distressing behavior that raises concerns about his or her personal well-being and often disrupts the campus community.

The Disturbed and Disturbing Student

Virginia L. Brown, David A. DeCoster

The combination of problematical student behaviors, intense campus pressures, and the potential for serious personal as well as institutional consequences causes decisions regarding disturbed/disturbing students to be highly complex and unpredictable. Assessment considerations are complicated, and the subsequent possibilities for appropriate interventions are many. Though all of these dynamics tend to defy meaningful description and planning, legal, medical, and educational authorities advise and even admonish administrators to provide specific and detailed written policies (Leach and Sewell, 1984; Pavela, 1985; Wagener, Sanders, and Thompson, 1982; and Gehring, 1983).

Applications of the Assessment-Intervention of Student Problems (AISP) model can be a useful tool in dealing with this complexity. The model assists in the recognition that disturbing behavior may be accompanied by psychological disturbance and vice versa. It also provides guidance for the selection of appropriate interventions. The need for a systematic approach to and use of the campus intervention team is especially important with disturbed/disturbing students, since attention to only one system is unlikely to resolve all the issues.

In this chapter, we will first briefly focus on "normal" development as a basis for understanding students with more intense and complex

U. Delworth (ed.). *Dealing with the Behavioral and Psychological Problems of Students.*
New Directions for Student Services, no. 45. San Francisco: Jossey-Bass, Spring 1989.

problems. We will then define and discuss assessment of the disturbed/disturbing students and move on to discuss effective interventions.

Developmental Framework

Before defining the disturbed/disturbing student, it is important to consider students in a broader context. Identification of the disturbed/disturbing student is not possible without an adequate understanding of what can be considered normal behavior. While allowing for individual differences in life history (for example, level of intelligence, personality, and socioeconomic status), it is reasonable to assume that the majority of traditional-age students will be largely concerned with identity development. According to Erikson (1950), the fifth of eight stages in individual psychosocial development is identity versus role confusion. The important question to be answered during this stage is How am I the same and how am I different? The goal for resolution of this stage is "the accrued confidence that the inner sameness and continuity prepared in the past are matched by the sameness and continuity of one's meaning for others, as evidenced in the tangible promise of a career" (pp. 261–262).

In the process of identity formation adolescents frequently engage in new and different behaviors. Some new behaviors are deviant, stemming from a need to try on new roles considered unacceptable by the larger society. Deviant behavior may also stem from a need for acceptance by one's peers. Depending on the peer group, this process also provides the opportunity for new behaviors that lead to success and positive resolution for this period of life crisis.

Assuming that entry into higher education typically occurs at a time of major developmental transition, that is, during the process of identity formation, and also assuming that this is a requisite task for every young person, knowledge about individual differences enhances understanding. In particular, it is helpful to view behavior from the perspective of each student's cognitive, emotional, and moral development. Several theorists (Harvey, Hunt, and Schroder, 1961; Kohlberg, 1969; Loevinger, 1976; Piaget, 1950; Perry, 1970) describe behavioral characteristics according to their assigned position along a continuum from concrete to abstract. Though this chapter forgoes a lengthy examination of theory, we wish to point out that all the theories agree that degree of concreteness or abstractness is related to one's ability to successfully negotiate life tasks and that certain predictable behavioral characteristics are manifest at certain points along the continuum. For example, the concrete person has a dualistic world view and uses absolute categories to aid an understanding of people, knowledge, and values. This person is likely to be egocentric, rigid, intolerant of ambiguity and, therefore, also intolerant of people who are different from himself or herself. Because the concrete person does not consider alternative viewpoints when assessing situations and events, fewer choices for behavioral responses are available. According to Schroder, Driver, and Streufert (1967), it is likely that this person will reach a last-resort response, such as aggression, more rapidly than the abstract person. Because of the concrete orientation, the central focus is on authority, and this has numerous implications for behavior.

In contrast to the concrete person, the abstract person perceives the world in relativistic terms. This person understands that there is rarely one right answer, but rather that *right* translates to better or best, and better or best can only be determined after consideration of all relevant information, including the consequences for self and others. The more abstract person is open to and even appreciative of the differences among people and is likely to respond with empathy.

The relevance of identity formation and cognitive, emotional, and moral development to the assessment of the disturbed/disturbing student is clear when we consider that the majority of students are both engaged in identity formation and more likely to be at a lower or concrete stage of development. This, of course, may not be so true of older students. However, these students may well be returning to identity issues as they assume or reassume the role of student. Behavior manifested by the student who is functioning at a lower, or concrete, stage of development may be misinterpreted. Depending on the nature and severity of the disturbed/disturbing behavior presented, it may be difficult to distinguish between those behaviors that are indicative of functional development and those resulting from psychological disorders.

The Disturbed/Disturbing Student

As Delworth states in Chapter One, any combination of disturbed and disturbing characteristics is possible. The key for using the disturbed/disturbing designation is that both aspects are prominent enough to require referral and intervention. For example, a student who seriously abuses alcohol (disturbed) may also cause damage to the property of others (disturbing). In a more extreme example, a student who believes an instructor has taken control of his or her mind (disturbed) may try to harm the instructor (disturbing). A key issue is that only one part of the problem, often the disturbing part, may be identified. As Delworth notes, disturbing behavior is more likely to be seen first in residence halls or by law enforcement officers. Disturbed behavior may be noticed by peers, faculty members, or anyone who has ongoing contact with the student. It is vital, then, for all relevant members of the campus community to have at least some rudimentary skills in assessing whether a student who is disturbing the campus environment is also in need of mental health services. In the opposite case, the possibility of disturbing behaviors on the part of clearly disturbed students must also be explored. Often, this additional exploration will take place in the context of either the judicial or the mental health system that is involved in the immediate presenting behavior.

The judicial process, the approach advocated by Ragle and Justice in Chapter Two of this volume, calls for further exploration of the student's cognitive and affective functioning. In the examples used by Ragle and Justice, problems in identity development and effective moral reasoning are identified. These developmental deficiencies can be handled well within the type of judicial process described by the authors. Such a process also allows for identification of problems that would be labeled disturbed. For example, Ragle and Justice's "Christine" might have had bizarre reasons for her cheating, or she might have had a severe alcohol problem or eating disorder that interfered with her academic work. In such cases, it would be appropriate to label her disturbed/disturbing and to broaden the resources and interventions used to help her.

McKinley and Dworkin's discussion of the assessment of disturbed students (Chapter Three) serves as a base for further exploration of disturbing behaviors as well. A prime example would be students who are identified as having a chemical dependency problem, since substance abuse is often associated with disturbing (and sometimes illegal) behaviors.

Severely disturbed/disturbing behavior, albeit easier to identify and encountered less often, has the potential for greater harm for a larger number of people. Consider, for example, the chilling and devastating impact of a campus homicide or suicide on both the institution and the surrounding community (Tanner and Sewell, 1977, 1978, and 1979). The tragic consequences of one disturbed person's behavior can create an instant climate of shock and fear that often brings chaos to the community. Though certainly the disturbed/disturbing student's actions do not always result in a sudden and violent death, the severely disturbed/disturbing student often presents concerns that cannot be ignored by administrators and educators. On one hand, concern for the student demands a response, and on the other, pressure from outraged students, their parents, and perhaps colleagues requires immediate attention.

According to a National Institute of Mental Health report (1972), the incidence of students who suffer psychotic episodes during college is between two and five per one thousand students. Thompson, Bentz, and Liptzin (1973) reported that a review of eleven major studies revealed rates of psychiatric disorders in the college population ranging from 6 percent to 16 percent. At Oregon State University, where uncooperative disturbed students are referred to a medical review board for evaluation, the following disturbing behaviors constituted the presenting problems for twenty-seven students over a twelve-year period (Wagener, Sanders, and Thompson, 1980): verbal homicidal threats, physical attacks on others, life-threatening self-destructive actions, severe disruption of educational and support systems, destruction of property, and exhibitionism. The resulting psychiatric evaluations revealed that all twenty-seven students fell into one of the following diagnostic categories: schizophrenic reaction, paranoid type; major affective disorder; personality disorder, antisocial behavior; anorexia nervosa; substance abuse disorder; and borderline personality.

The findings of the Oregon Medical Review Board raise two important issues. The first is that the small numbers should help us to keep the problem in its proper perspective. The second issue is that these students were clearly disturbed/disturbing, and they were not grappling with the typical developmental problems of young adults. Similarly, their behavior would not improve merely by improving their interpersonal relationships with peers. They were suffering from the type of acute emotional disorder that requires astute mental health treatment.

Decision Making Within the AISP Model

The AISP model provides for a campus intervention team to make an assessment regarding disturbed/disturbing students and to help make recommendations for appropriate interventions. Though it is recognized that a multidimensional approach—that is, utilizing more than one intervention either simultaneously or sequentially—may be advantageous, reviewing the potential options individually seems most appropriate.

Judicial System. Pavela (1982, 1985) argues feverishly in favor of utilizing disciplinary or judicial systems rather than relying on forced psychiatric or medical withdrawal policies—referring to the latter as "therapeutic paternalism." Administrators, he maintains, tend to misuse withdrawal policies to avoid judicial procedures that are unduly cumbersome and legalistic. Furthermore, administrators often fail to understand the inherent value of the disciplinary process in fostering moral development and ethical standards: "If the student lacks the capacity to respond to the disciplinary charges or did not know the nature and wrongfulness of the act in question" (Pavela, 1985, p. 61).

Though many disturbed/disturbing students might appropriately be held accountable for behavior that violates institutional or community standards, there may be additional circumstances that challenge the wisdom of referrals to the judicial system for some of these students. Judicial procedures of due process are sometimes viewed by severely disturbed/disturbing students as tedious and superficial. They might perceive board members at the hearing as pawns of the administration, and they may believe that persons giving testimony have a personal grudge against them. In addition, judicial board members are most often volunteers from the campus community who have little experience with emotional disorders and may themselves be intimidated, fear some sort of retaliation from the student, or simply feel incompetent to respond in ways that are appropriate or helpful. Thus the interaction of such dynamics may cause the campus intervention team to evaluate the potential impact of referring a disturbed/disturbing student to the judicial system. The team must ask whether the experience is likely to be in the best interest of the student and the institution, or whether it is more likely to aggravate existing problems. A decision to circumvent the judicial system in some cases must be acknowledged as a reasonable and appropriate option that may expedite a favorable resolution for the student, family members, and the victimized persons within the campus community. Utilizing a mediation process as advocated by Serr and Taber (1987) is one alternative to the traditional judicial system that has been useful in resolving problems involving disturbed students.

Mental Health System. The mental health system encompasses resources far broader than the offerings of the college or university, and procedural requirements are ultimately determined by individual state statutes. Depending on the availability of university personnel, community resources may also be utilized.

McKinley and Dworkin (in Chapter Three of this volume) outline various ways in which the mental health system can serve disturbed students. Psychiatric emergencies and determination of the need for commitment to a mental health facility are two components that warrant further discussion, since disturbed/disturbing students are the most likely category within the AISP model to require such responses. Policies and procedures for handling psychiatric emergencies must be known by student affairs educators as well as by medical personnel and law enforcement authorities. Obviously, a system designed to respond to student psychiatric emergencies will vary according to campus resources. However, mental health professionals must be on call and available to ensure that the student receives appropriate treatment in the most expeditious manner possible. For example, during regular office hours, a staff member of the mental health facility should respond to a psychiatric emergency directly. After hours, a prerecorded telephone message can direct the caller to the campus health center, campus police, or some other office that has access to a list of mental health professionals on call for immediate consultation. Depending on the severity of the situation, the mental health professional can advise appropriate action or communicate directly with the student either by telephone or in person. Should the psychiatric emergency be first discovered at a local hospital emergency room, an evaluation and disposition under normal protocol is appropriate. If the student is admitted to the hospital, the campus mental health professional should be contacted immediately for consultation or on the next day for follow up. The emergency-room physician should also have the option of consultation with an on-call university mental health professional to assist in decision making regarding the following disposition options: release, hospitalization, and referral to a state psychiatric facility for evaluation.

Procedures, requirements, and regulations for commitment to a mental health facility are determined by state law in order to protect individual rights and ensure appropriate and effective treatment. In the case of involuntary commitment, a campus mental health professional should remain involved as necessary to assist the student in the appropriate voluntary withdrawal process or future reentry to the education system. This professional, or another university staff member, must also ensure due process for the student.

Involuntary mental health commitment is initiated through legal procedures and varies according to individual state statutes. This determination is based on a judgment that the person is dangerous to self or others. The following excerpt from a Pennsylvania statute is offered to provide clarity:

> The standards of clear and present danger may be met when a person has made a threat of harm to self or others, has made a threat to commit suicide, or has made a threat to commit an act of mutilation and has committed acts in furtherance of any such threats. . . . When the petition for commitment filed under section 301 (b) (2) (i) alleges that a person poses a clear and present danger to himself or herself, clinical or other testimony may be considered which demonstrates that the person's judgment and insight is so severely impaired that he or she is engaging in uncontrollable behavior which is so grossly irrational or grossly inappropriate to the situation that such behavior prevents him or her from satisfying a need for reasonable nourishment, personal care, medical care, shelter or self-protection and safety, and that serious physical debilitation, serious bodily injury, or death may occur within thirty days unless adequate treatment is provided on an involuntary basis [Commonwealth of Pennsylvania, 1984, p. 5100–45].

In the case of involuntary commitment, the campus mental health professional should be available for consultation and, if appropriate, to facilitate a voluntary withdrawal from the institution. The process of commitment is discussed here as one option in a total mental health system. However, it is important to keep in mind that this process occurs independent of the campus and, in fact, might not be known by the campus community. This brings us to a crucial issue related to the role of the campus mental health professional in facilitating a student's withdrawal.

Campus mental health professionals are responsible primarily to act in the best interest of the student. Disturbance of the student's environment is an important consideration when deciding whether to remove a student from the college. A decision to remove the student from the campus environment is an administrative function determined either by appropriate campus authorities or by local community authorities. For example, though the campus mental health professional may have established a relationship with the student and so be influential in facilitating a voluntary withdrawal from the college, this same professional should not be a member of an institutional decision-making body assembled to make withdrawal determinations unless specifically requested to participate by the client or otherwise allowed to do so through a signed consent form.

Utilizing the campus intervention team, a representative from the mental health system would be appropriately involved to develop and approve policy related to assessment and assignment of students to such specific campus systems as judicial, mental health, or both. The mental health professional can be particularly helpful in advising administrators regarding students who might be harmed by entry into the judicial system. It is important, however, for a clear distinction to be made between the mental health professional in this administrative role and the mental health professional in the role of personal therapist in order to protect the student's right to privacy and not interfere with future treatment. Caution must be observed to ensure confidentiality when establishing the campus intervention team so that the value of the mental health system is not diminished and perceived by students as watchdog for the administration.

Campus Treatment Intervention

The campus intervention team is probably most important for the student classified as disturbed/disturbing. According to the AISP model, this student will probably become involved in both the mental health and the judicial system and has the greatest potential for invoking withdrawal determinations. As was pointed out both in the section on judicial systems and in the section on mental health systems, some students not only may not profit from entry into a judicial system but they may be agitated or harmed as a result. Therefore, when assessment and determination is made for the disturbed/disturbing student by the campus intervention team, these circumstances should receive great consideration. It must be emphasized that a well-functioning campus intervention team should contribute greatly to the best possible outcome for the disturbed/disturbing student.

Some disturbed/disturbing students who end up withdrawing or being dismissed from a university that has a fragmented system might not have come to such a point if they had had the benefit of an astute campus intervention team. For example, consider the type A disturbing student who is exhibiting many immature behaviors such as playing pranks in the residence hall, destroying other students' property, cutting classes, being easily frustrated and agitated, and overreacting to minor problems. Consider further, that this student also manifests behaviors associated with type B disturbed behavior (for example, the student is overly rigid, demonstrates highly dualistic thinking, and is angry and destructive toward others).

In a fragmented system, this student would probably be referred either to the judicial system or to the mental health system, depending on which staff member makes the referral and under what circumstances. Obviously, people interpret behavior differently. However, a more effective outcome might be reached by the campus intervention team. Recognizing that the disturbed/disturbing behavior might result from a difficult adjustment to college for a student functioning at a lower level of cognitive and emotional development, the team might refer the student to the counseling center, where he or she could receive therapy and establish at least one meaningful relationship. As this intervention progresses, other campus interventions can be invoked as needed to facilitate the student's developmental growth (for example, academic counseling, communication-skills building, and a peer support group). At the same time, the type of judicial process advocated by Ragle and Justice might help such students accept the consequences of their behavior.

This is not to deny the fact that the severely disturbed/disturbing student may be best served by leaving the educational system through involuntary or voluntary withdrawal. It is also conceivable, however, that the campus team could expedite an appropriate withdrawal in a more humane manner.

Withdrawal and Dismissal

Terms like *psychiatric separation* (Zirkel and Bargerstock, 1980), *mandatory psychological evaluations* or *forced counseling* (Gibbs and Campbell, 1984), and *involuntary medical withdrawal* (Wagener, Sanders, and Thompson, 1982) all bring to mind an unwelcome and unhappy set of circumstances. Our general disdain for such situations is understandable, as the impetus for each action stems from the same uncomfortable source: the realization that another human being is being coerced into doing something against his or her will. It is not surprising then, that most educators find it difficult to participate in such a decision, and they are reluctant to communicate or impose the authority necessary for implementation. Most of us share this deep apprehension as well as the feeling that these actions infringe on basic and sacred human rights. In the case of disturbed/disturbing students, anxiety may be heightened by the knowledge that their behavior is unpredictable and the expectation that the decision is likely to create an emotional, hysterical, or perhaps violent reaction. To minimize the possibility that this type of power might be used arbitrarily, we are advised to write policies carefully and develop procedures that reflect an appreciation for individual rights as well as concern for the campus community. Thus the imposition of an involuntary withdrawal is a difficult and controversial intervention that deserves more detailed review and discussion. To this end, it might be helpful to begin with a somewhat typical policy statement currently at Indiana University of Pennsylvania (IUP) and published in the student handbook as follows:

Involuntary Withdrawal Policy

The university community occasionally faces the problem of students who pose a threat to themselves or others, who are unable to cope with their own needs, or who create a pattern of extreme disruption. If such behavior constitutes a violation of university rules or regulations, the case will be referred to the university judicial system for action.

If the student's behavior occurs in the absence of any violation of rule or regulation, the vice-president for student affairs will investigate the situation and the effect of behavior on the student and the university community. The vice-president may require a personal interview with the student. If, as a result of this investigation, the vice-president determines that the student's withdrawal from campus may be necessary, he or she will recommend a withdrawal to the student. If the student will not withdraw voluntarily, the vice-president will consult with the Committee on Involuntary Withdrawal to advise him or her in the disposition of the case. The committee will consist of the student's dean or department chairperson and a representative from both the Health Center and the Counseling and Student Development Center. Neither representative should have had direct professional contact with the student. The committee will recommend to the vice-president a course of action, which may include involuntary withdrawal of the student from campus with conditions for readmission.

Students who leave campus under the above conditions, either voluntarily or involuntarily, will be readmitted to the university only after being cleared by the vice-president for student affairs with concurrence of the dean of the school enrolled. Permission for readmission will typically be based on the student's demonstrating a period of stable behavior outside the university and may require a statement from a physician, psychologist, or other qualified professional that the student is ready to return and cope with the stresses of university life. Conditions for follow-up services may be required as part of the readmission decision.

It is understood that involuntary withdrawal of a student from the campus will be undertaken only as a last resort. Every effort will be made to help students understand the consequences of their behavior, make responsible decisions, and develop skills that will allow them to function in the IUP community ["The Eye," 1986, p. 68].

Though perhaps not a perfect model, the statement is relatively clear and concise given the complexity and importance of the issue. The policy states in straightforward terms the criteria used to define the problem behavior: posing a threat to self or others (for example, suicide attempt, assault, and threats of physical violence), inability to cope with their own needs (for example, eating disorders, failure to follow the instructions of a physician or to take prescribed medication, which results in the student becoming physically or psychologically incapacitated), and creating a *pattern* of disruption (for example, property damage, bizarre or psychotic behavior). It might be argued that the types of behavior are described in terms that are too vague and thus allow for differing interpretations. The parenthetical examples are offered as potential causes for concern and not meant to imply that all such circumstances would trigger procedures leading to a decision regarding withdrawal. Pavela (1985) suggests that students who directly or substantially impeded the lawful activities of others could be candidates for further evaluation. Whatever descriptive statements are used, there will remain a need for some interpretation or judgment regarding whether or not the behavior meets the criteria.

It must also be understood that the institution has the obligation to demonstrate that the behavior in question does, in fact, create danger or disruption. The First Amendment gives students the right to freedom of expression, and Section 504 of the Rehabilitation Act of 1973 protects students from being dismissed simply because they have a mental disorder or behave in ways that might be considered strange, bizarre, or eccentric (Zirkel and Bargerstock, 1980). One student affairs administrator argued persistently that the institution was not equipped to treat a disturbed/disturbing student and that therefore, it should insist on an involuntary withdrawal. A frustrated psychiatrist finally said, "You don't seem to understand what I've been telling you. In our society crazy people have rights even when they happen to be students!"

The policy also provides for a possible referral to the judicial system when a violation of institutional regulations has occurred. It further specifies that the vice-president for student affairs should continue to investigate the situation if the behavior is not considered a violation of rules and regulations. We feel, however, that this limitation may be ill-advised, in that disturbing behavior that would ordinarily be confronted through disciplinary procedures might be more appropriately resolved in other ways—especially when there is potential for extreme disruption or physical violence. At any rate, if the vice-president chooses to pursue the matter, a personal interview with the student becomes part of the investigation. In actuality, the vice-president, as well as other administrators and educators, may have had multiple contacts with the student at this point as well as consultations with mental health professionals, parents, and legal counsel. This investigation may lead to the recommendation that the student voluntarily withdraw from school in order to seek treatment that might stabilize the condition and help to ensure a successful return to school. If a voluntary withdrawal is unacceptable to the student, the vice-president seeks more formal advice by convening an ad hoc committee on involuntary withdrawal and is guided by their recommendations. This group functions much in the same way as the campus intervention team described in the AISP model.

This process provides some elements of procedural due process that could be further strengthened by opportunities for the student to challenge and respond to the committee's findings or any psychological evaluations utilized. Students should be advised that they may be accompanied by a parent, friend, or legal counsel, although traditional adversarial procedures used in disciplinary hearings are neither necessary nor advised. Finally, students should receive a written statement that summarizes the investigation, the decision of the vice-president, and the conditions that are required for readmission. Typically, the vice-president requests that a university psychologist or psychiatrist evaluate the student by personally interviewing him or her and by studying any information that the student provides from independently chosen medical and mental health professionals familiar with the case.

Conclusion

Steele, Johnson, and Rickard (1984) found that 81 percent of a national sample of postsecondary institutions reported that some students had undergone involuntarily withdrawal resulting from psychiatric problems. Though the practice was generally utilized very sparingly (40 percent of the schools expelled two students over a two-year period), a cluster of seven institutions had expelled an average of 13.3 students during the same time period.

In a similar study Wagener, Sanders, and Thompson (1982) found that 58 percent of a sample of Pacific Coast College Health Association members reported that they had excluded or restricted the enrollment of students having serious emotional problems. But only a small number of students were affected: a mean of 3.15 students were expelled during one academic year. The actual numbers ranged from 0 to 25 students. This indicates that at least one institution, which expelled 25 students, utilized the policy to a much greater extent than most schools.

Both of these studies, then, suggest that some institutions are infringing on students' rights. Thus the fear expressed by Pavela (1982) that some administrators misuse and rely too heavily on a policy of involuntary withdrawal may be justified. If accurate, this unfortunate and uninformed practice denies students their constitutional rights and preempts the utilization of other interventions that may be helpful to them and could avoid a disruption of their education. Student affairs educators have an obligation not only to be knowledgeable but also to promote policy development and decision-making practices that are healthy and ethical. A greater degree of sensitivity and courage may well be needed in relating to disturbed/disturbing students who are already experiencing stress and vulnerability.

References

Commonwealth of Pennsylvania. *Pennsylvania Code.* Title 55 5100.84. Public Welfare. Mechanicsburg, Pa.: Fry Communications, 1984.

Erikson, E. H. *Childhood and Society.* New York: Norton, 1950.

"The Eye." Student Handbook. Indiana, Pa.: Indiana University of Pennsylvania, 1986.

Gehring, D. "The Dismissal of Students with Serious Emotional Problems: An Administrative Decision Model." *NASPA Journal,* 1983, *21,* 9–14.

Gibbs, A., and Campbell, J. M. "Mandatory Psychological Evaluations: A Balance Between Conflicting Interests." *Journal of College Student Personnel,* 1984, *25,* 115–121.

Harvey, O. J., Hunt, D. E., and Schroder, H. M. *Conceptual Systems and Personality Organization.* New York: Wiley, 1961.

Kohlberg, L. "Stage and Sequence: The Cognitive Development Approach to Socialization." In D. A. Goslin (ed.), *Handbook of Socialization Theory and Research.* Chicago: Rand McNally, 1969.

Leach, B. E., and Sewell, J. D. "Responding to Students with Mental Disorders: A Framework for Action." *NASPA Journal,* 1984, *22,* 37–43.

Loevinger, J. *Ego Development: Conceptions and Theories.* San Francisco: Jossey-Bass, 1976.

National Institute of Mental Health. *Facts About College Mental Health.* Washington, D.C.: Superintendent of Documents, U.S. Government Printing Office, 1972.

Pavela, G. "Therapeutic Paternalism and the Misuse of Mandatory Psychiatric Withdrawals on Campus." *Journal of College and University Law,* 1982, *9,* 101–141.

Pavela, G. *The Dismissal of Students with Mental Disorders: Legal Issues, Policy Considerations, and Alternative Responses.* Asheville, N.C.: College Administration Publications, 1985.

Perry, W. G. *Forms of Intellectual and Ethical Development in the College Years: A Scheme.* New York: Holt, Rinehart & Winston, 1970.

Piaget, J. *The Psychology of Intelligence.* San Diego, Calif.: Harcourt Brace Jovanovich, 1950.

Schroder, H. M., Driver, M. H., and Streufert, S. *Human Information Processing.* New York: Holt, Rinehart & Winston, 1967.

Serr, R. L., and Taber, R. S. "Mediation: A Judicial Affairs Alternative." In R.

Caruso and W. W. Travelstead (eds.), *Enhancing Campus Judicial Systems*. New Directions for Student Services, no. 38. San Francisco: Jossey-Bass, 1987.

Steele, B. H., Johnson, H. D., and Rickard, S. T. "Managing the Judicial Function in Student Affairs." *Journal of College Student Personnel*, 1984, *25*, 337–342.

Tanner, W. A., and Sewell, J. D. "University Mental Health Problems: An Alternative Approach." *Campus Law Enforcement Journal*, 1977, *7*, 15–17.

Tanner, W. A., and Sewell, J. D. "Campus Homicide: One University's Administrative Response." *Campus Law Enforcement Journal*, 1978, *8*, 25–28.

Tanner, W. A., and Sewell, J. D. "The University Response Team: An Assessment." *Campus Law Enforcement Journal*, 1979, *9*, 28–31.

Thompson, J. R., Bentz, W. K., and Liptzin, M. B. "The Prevalence of Psychiatric Disorders in an Undergraduate Population." *College Health*, 1973, *21*, 415–422.

Wagener, J. M., Sanders, R. S., and Thompson, G. E. "Modifying Student Status Due to Emotional Illness: The Role of the Medical Review Board." Paper presented at the Pacific Coast College Health Association, October 1980.

Wagener, J. M., Sanders, R. S., and Thompson, G. E. "Reacting to the Uncooperative Severely Disturbed Student: A Survey of Health Center Policies." Paper presented at the Research Symposium, American College Health Association, April 1982.

Zirkel, P. A., and Bargerstock, C. T. "Two Current Legal Concerns in College Student Affairs: Alcohol Consumption and Psychiatric Separation." *Journal of College Student Personnel*, 1980, *21*, 252–256.

Virginia L. Brown is director of the Center for Community Affairs at Indiana University of Pennsylvania and has served in a variety of teaching and administrative positions in the mental health field.

David A. DeCoster is vice-president for student affairs at Indiana University of Pennsylvania and serves as associate editor for the Journal of College Student Development *of the American College Personnel Association.*

The responsibilities of chief student affairs officers for the resolution of student problems are discussed. The AISP model is considered as a structured approach for use by institutions.

A Chief Student Affairs Officer's Perspective on the AISP Model

Arthur Sandeen

Among the most important goals of any student affairs program is to assist students who are experiencing personal problems. Established, residential institutions with traditional-age students are likely to have more day-to-day contact with their students than their counterparts at urban commuter institutions and thus may devote more extensive resources to personal support services. But even at colleges and universities with part-time, older, and commuting students, there is a need to respond in positive ways to students' personal problems. Such services are often offered because of student-consumer demand, faculty or parental pressure, and attrition-retention problems, but they are also offered because the institution has a sincere desire to help its students.

It is the responsibility of the chief student affairs officer to understand the needs of the campus; to know which kinds of services and programs will meet these needs; to convince the faculty, president, and governing board that these services are needed; and to find the necessary resources for them. These responsibilities are required for all of the programs in the student affairs division, and the dean or vice-president must be able to articulate these programs and communicate their importance to the

U. Delworth (ed.). *Dealing with the Behavioral and Psychological Problems of Students.*
New Directions for Student Services, no. 45. San Francisco: Jossey-Bass, Spring 1989.

academic community. Moreover, it is the dean's or the vice-president's responsibility to see that the programs are implemented, that they operate according to plan, and that they are systematically evaluated.

On virtually every campus, the needs and demands for services exceed the available resources. This is as true in student affairs as it is in academic, research, development, and financial affairs programs. As a result, chief student affairs officers spend a significant part of their time and energy competing for available campus resources. The success of an institution's student affairs program is often a reflection of the ability of the chief student affairs officer to win the trust and confidence of faculty members, administrators, and students, and sometimes the student affairs staff itself. The dean or vice-president must have not only a clear notion of the division's priorities but also a realistic understanding of what the faculty and the administration will agree to.

Within this context, the chief student affairs officer should know the extent to which students are experiencing serious personal problems, the current resources and policies directed at these problems, and the likelihood that other administrators will accept his or her approach to them. The Assessment-Intervention of Student Problems (AISP) model represents a thoughtful approach to addressing student problems from the perspective of a chief student affairs officer. In the following sections questions are presented and discussed regarding the AISP model.

Is the Model Useful and Workable?

The AISP model represents the general strategy already followed by many institutions, and it can be very useful because of its clarity, simplicity, and emphasis on coordination. It is also quite understandable to those outside the student affairs division.

One of the principal concerns of chief student affairs officers when handling student problems is that often there does not seem to be any systematic plan. The staff responds day after day to problems as they present themselves, and on each occasion, staff members seem to be operating on an ad hoc basis. The AISP model, however, clearly defines responsibilities and establishes procedures to follow. Moreover, it flows from a sound propostion—that assessment and intervention are needed in order to address student problems in workable ways.

Assessment of disturbed or disturbing students is never an exact science, and the informal nature of the assessment process in the AISP model is a recognition of this reality. Often it is the residence-hall staff, or those most closely associated with students, who are in the best position to make initial assessments. Many campuses have hired and trained undergraduate students as peer advisers, working under the direction of the counseling center, to assist in the identification of students with personal problems. Such a program is easily included in the AISP model. Other, more elaborate and formal methods of student assessment can be implemented as well, especially in conjunction with orientation programs and general education classes.

Perhaps the most attractive feature of the AISP model for a chief student affairs administrator is the coordination it ensures among the various offices (student services, mental health, security, legal, and judicial officer). Though these offices work together by necessity on most campuses, too often coordination is not done in the systematic manner suggested by the AISP model. Frequently, one or more of the offices is not involved or is overlooked in the rush of activity that is often associated with the handling of such problems. Even though the staff members in these offices may be familiar with each other, the model can probably be strengthened if a leader or coordinator for the intervention team is designated. This would establish clear responsibility, and the chief student affairs officer would have no doubt about whom to contact for information. The intervention team may want to avoid being publicized on campus as such, since most students do not want to be known as the target of any such group.

When it is decided that intervention is needed, the model proves to be quite sound. A chief student affairs officer, when handling disturbed and disturbing students, needs to be assured that staff members have made a competent decision regarding the situation. By involving more than one office or staff person in this process, the probability of making a good decision is clearly increased. Moreover, the participation by other staff members helps to solve a problem that troubles many chief student affairs administratorrs—the tendency for some staff members to avoid making difficult decisions regarding problem students. The participation of the team in the assessment-intervention process may give support and encouragement to staff members who are very close to students on a daily basis but who hesitate to take necessary action.

Can the Institution Afford This Level of Individual Attention to Student Problems?

There are many of good programs and services that student affairs divisions would like to offer, but with limited financial and staff resources, priorities have to be established, and only a portion of the programs can be adopted. This, of course, is one of the most important and difficult responsibilities of the chief student affairs administrator. In their zeal to respond to the needs of the campus, some student affairs administrators have failed by spreading their programs too thin, trying to do too many things with limited resources. This inevitably results in poor performance, lack of follow up, and dissatisfied customers. Nothing can damage a student affairs program more than programs that are viewed as low in quality by students and faculty.

It is the responsibility of the chief student affairs officer to understand the president's priorities for the institution's student affairs program. Much of his or her time is devoted to informing the president (and other key administrators) about these priorities, but it is necessary to conduct programs and services that match the goals of the institution. When the activities of the student affairs division are out of sync with the priorities of the institution, it is very likely that new leadership for the student affairs program will be found. This is an important point in evaluating the AISP model on any campus. At some colleges, there is not only a tradition but a clear expectation that the institution will devote a lot of time (and thus services) to the personal problems of students. On others, there are other priorities (such as financial aid or placement) that are considered more important. This institutional assessment of priorities is a key responsibility of the chief student affairs officer.

No matter what the priorities of the institution, it is clear that the AISP model is expensive. Often many full-time (and probably some part-time) staff members must spend their time on the needs and problems of one student. On some campuses, this may be a luxury that simply cannot be afforded. Moreover, the chief student affairs officer must decide exactly how much disruptive behavior the university will tolerate from disturbed and disturbing students. Should valuable staff time be spent on resolving the problems of a small number of troublesome students while the needs of the vast majority go unmet?

The AISP model can be viewed in another manner as well, however. If the staff is committed to it, the model can actually result in some economies for the student affairs division. With the clear assessment-intervention approach, it may be likely that quicker resolutions of problems with these students will take place, freeing the staff to spend more time on programs for the majority of students. A worrisome issue for many chief student affairs officers is deciding how much staff time should be devoted to therapeutic care. Most campuses cannot afford to provide long-term psychological support for individual students, and the AISP model is very helpful in addressing this problem. In effect, the model requires decision making through systematic assessment and intervention. This feature of the model is attractive to chief student affairs administrators, some of whom are impatient over the reluctance of some staff members to make decisions regarding problem students.

Of course, priorities for student affairs programs are not determined solely on the basis of economy. For the chief student affairs officer who is convinced that his or her institution needs to express more humane concern for students with personal problems, the AISP model can be quite helpful. It can help demonstrate to others that the institution does care about individual students and that such caring can have very positive consequences. Chief student affairs officers are often viewed as "bleeding hearts" by their administrative colleagues (and some board members), and the kind of systematic assessment-intervention used in the AISP model can produce results that are objective and compelling.

On large campuses, there may be so many disturbed or disturbing students that four or five intervention teams are necessary. This involves more staff time but may be the only way to get the job done. Frequent involvement in these problems can result in burnout for staff members, so having several teams and shifting assignments of staff members can help prevent such problems. On small campuses, the team may consist of two student affairs staff members, a faculty volunteer, and an older student-paraprofessional. Few small institutions have enough full-time professional staff members to form a five-member intervention team within its student affairs division.

An institution that decides it cannot afford the resources required to address the problems of disturbed and disturbing students may discover that the costs of ignoring them are too great. If students have had experiences at a college and leave with a very negative attitude toward it, the institution has not served them well, and the college may develop a reputation of being an uncaring, impersonal institution. In this regard, the AISP model may help the chief student affairs administrator move the institution toward a humane yet decisive approach to the personal problems of students. In the long run, this may be a very economical strategy for the institution.

How Can the Model Be Linked to Faculty and Academic Departments?

Most chief student affairs administrators know that the quickest way to lose funding for a program is to isolate it from others outside the student affairs division. This is especially true with the faculty. If the AISP model is to be successful, it needs the awareness and support of the faculty, and this is one of the primary responsibilities of the chief student affairs administrator.

If students are disturbed or disturbing, they are likely to display such behavior in more than one setting. If faculty members are aware of the support services provided by the student affairs division, and have confidence in them, they can be a tremendous asset to the resolution of problems. Students acting out their negative behavior in the residence halls may also do so in the classroom or laboratory. In order to make the AISP model successful, the student affairs staff should meet with academic deans, department chairs, and the faculty senate to explain the program and ask for their support. It is primarily through this personal contact with faculty members that their support will be gained. The provost or chief academic affairs officer can be of significant help as well, and the student affairs administrator should ensure that he or she is contacted.

Some student affairs divisions have formed formal faculty advisory committees, and these groups often prove valuable in gaining support for programs such as the AISP model. Moreover, suggestions from faculty groups can result in real program improvements. Faculty members who become better informed about useful ways of helping students with personal problems can become great assets to the student affairs division. No student affairs staff is large enough to address all the problems on its campus, and faculty members are the most valuable resource available to them.

The intervention team suggested in the AISP model could probably be strengthened in many cases by the inclusion of a faculty member, especially one from the student's major department. Before such participation can take place, however, the student affairs staff has to inform faculty members about the program and convince them that their support is important to its success.

What Other Resources May Be Available to the Student Affairs Staff?

For students who live on campus, staff members from the various departments can come together to form a helping team for disturbed or disturbing students. In many cases, however, the majority of the students live off campus, and the model may not fit as neatly. The chief student affairs officer should be aware of the various support services in the community, should initiate contacts with them, and should encourage the staff to use them.

Even though students may live in private apartments and rooming houses off campus, there are often resident managers of these facilities who can be supportive of the student affairs staff. By making efforts to consult with them over a period of time, the student affairs staff will find that they can often be of considerable assistance. Newsletters can include information about how and where to seek help for students experiencing problems. Often, a telephone crisis line can prove helpful to students living off campus. Student-paraprofessionals can be hired to live in major off-campus apartments, and these off-campus residence assistants can be a very valuable link to the student affairs staff.

For students experiencing difficult problems, it is not unlikely for the police to become involved. In most communities, police departments are eager to participate in educational programs designed to help young people, and their participation in the intervention team can be an asset, especially concerning students living off campus. It should be the responsibility of the chief student affairs officer to arrange such cooperative participation.

Among the most effective groups in assisting the student affairs staff with difficult students is the local clergy. At most colleges and universities, several members of the clergy are assigned specifically to minister to students. They often have special insights regarding student problems and may have helpful connections to the student's family and home community. The clergy can, when appropriate, participate as a member of the AISP intervention team.

The chief student affairs officer should also be very familiar with the various community-based helping services. In fact, it would be unusual for an active chief student affairs administrator not to be involved directly with these community services, frequently in a leadership capacity. If the professionals who work in community mental health, drug and alcohol abuse programs, and family services are in close contact with the institution's student affairs staff, there will be many opportunities to work together to help students with serious problems. This is especially important, of course, at institutions where a large proportion of the students live off campus. Community service professionals often deal with serious personal problems and can be very helpful to the student affairs staff.

What Implications Does the AISP Model Have
for the Student Affairs Staff?

The chief student affairs officer should always be seeking ways of helping staff members perform their job more effectively. Few institutions can afford to allow Ph.D.-level staff members to have only five or six individual student contacts per day, and thus professional staff members in student affairs are increasingly viewed as generators of multiple activities, through the use of teaching assistants, volunteers, paraprofessionals, faculty members, and other part-time helpers. Moreover, experienced student affairs professionals, like senior faculty members, are often expected to attract the financial resources necessary to implement various programs. One of the important new challenges for chief student affairs officers is to encourage (and convince) senior staff members in their divisions to become grant and project managers. Within this context, the AISP model is still viewed as very helpful and workable, but it is unlikely that senior student affairs staff members will become direct participants on the intervention team. Their role must be to adequately prepare and supervise those on their staffs who are on the team. This transition from direct participant to supervisor-manager of paraprofessionals and others may be a difficult one for some experienced student affairs professionals to make, but it is a necessary one in terms of financial constraints.

Perhaps the most attractive feature of the AISP model is the cooperation it requires among staff members. It has the potential to encourage the various departments to work together, countering the tendency for some one department to covet a program as exclusively its own. Therefore, the AISP model frees chief student affairs officers from devoting so much time convincing various staff members to work together.

When staff members from several departments are involved in an intervention team, another likely outcome is that this contact will lead to productive new ideas. Especially on large campuses, staff members in one department are often so engrossed in their own concerns that they do not realize how they could increase their effectiveness by working with others. The AISP model is very helpful in this regard. Indeed, it may be an effective way of testing the ability and willingness of staff members to work together.

The AISP model assumes that the student affairs staff is responsible for intervening when students cause serious problems for themselves or others. Moreover, it assumes that the student affairs staff is responsible for taking action to solve the problems. This active, managing role may be resisted by some staff members, who may have been accustomed to playing a more passive role in the past. These staff members may believe that to impose "solutions" on students, often against their will, is unprofessional and counterproductive. These views must be weighed carefully against the needs and rights of other members of the academic community whose lives may be affected by disturbed or disturbing students. The chief student affairs officer should be sensitive to the varied perspectives that inevitably exist among the staff, and he or she must develop a policy approach that meets the needs of the particular campus. At most colleges and universities of the late 1980s, chief student affairs administrators are expected to solve problems, and the AISP model is supportive of this expectation.

How Does the Chief Student Affairs Officer Gauge the Success of the AISP Model?

The AISP model is attractive in terms of effecting staff coordination, emphasizing assessment and intervention, and insisting on decision making. But how does the chief student affairs officer know that the model is working or that students are actively being helped?

In order to assess the effectiveness of the AISP model, accurate information must be provided. How many disturbed and disturbing students have been contacted? What actions have been taken? What are the age, race, sex, academic major, and address of each problem student? What has the reaction been to others living, working, or studying with the student after contact has been made? What has happened to the student after contact with the crisis team and its interventions in terms of personal adjustment and academic achievement? What do the staff members involved in the process think of the model? The answers to these questions can provide the basis on which the AISP model can be evaluated. If the actual results are not very encouraging, especially in relation to the approach the staff had taken before adopting the AISP model, then the chief student affairs administrator needs to decide if the model is worth retaining. Adequate time is necessary to get an accurate assessment of the model. After an academic year's experience with it, a fair idea of its usefulness can probably be obtained.

Of course, the most important criterion in evaluating the effectiveness of the model is the extent to which it has helped the students. However, even this goal needs to be viewed in light of how much time the staff is able to spend on these problems. Most student affairs programs do not see their primary role as therapeutic or corrective, and if the AISP model results in staff members' spending a lot of time on these problems, the chief student affairs officer may have to make some changes. This is a familiar dilemma for all student affairs administrators. The majority of the students need efficient services and leadership programs, whereas a very small number with serious problems consume a disproportionate amount of staff time and energy. The particular needs of the institution and the president's expectations for the student affairs division will be the major factors in determining the actions taken by the chief student affairs administrator.

Strategies for assisting disturbed and disturbing students vary from one campus to another. The chief student affairs officer can review these other approaches and compare them with the AISP mode. It may be helpful after the first year's experience with the model to schedule a staff-faculty seminar to discuss the effort. A consultant from another campus, who is familiar with the AISP model as well as with other approaches, could be invited to join the seminar.

The AISP model is worthy of careful consideration by student affairs administrators, as it offers a clearly defined way of addressing real student problems. Moreover, it holds promise because it requires staff members to work together and make decisions designed to help troubled students and those affected by them. The AISP model is understandable to others outside of student affairs, and it can easily be adapted to include the faculty, community service personnel, campus ministers, and others. From the viewpoint of a chief student affairs administrator, the AISP model offers a workable way of dealing with problems that have caused significant difficulty for colleges and universities for many years.

*Arthur Sandeen is the vice-president for student affairs at
the University of Florida, where he is also a professor of
educational leadership. He served as president of NASPA
in 1977–78 and chaired the ACE-NASPA committee that wrote*
A Perspective on Student Affairs, *published in 1987.*

For minority students, the Assessment-Intervention of Student Problems model necessitates greater cultural awareness on the part of faculty and staff. The campus intervention team called for by the model would provide much needed support for students who may not readily use traditional resources.

Minority Students and the AISP Model

Paul Shang

The Assessment-Intervention of Student Problems (AISP) model assigns the assessment of student problems to all staff members who interact with students. Younger workers such as residence-hall staff members, who may have more informal interaction with students, share assessment responsibilities with faculty members who, at large, research-oriented institutions, may have less contact with individual students.

If the AISP model is to work with Hispanic, black, Native American, and Asian-American students, staff members responsible for assessment must be knowledgeable of differing cultural, economic, and educational backgrounds of the students, and of the effects of the campus environment on the students.

Of equal importance is the introduction of students to the services available at their institution, the studying and coping skills necessary for success, the mores of their particular educational community, and the behavior that is expected of them from the beginning of their enrollment. Early-orientation programs for minority students should include such services as financial aid counseling, assessment of skills and academic preparation, career counseling, and academic advising, which may lead to placing students in enrichment or remedial course work (Christoffel, 1986). However, without discussing how students from different cultural

U. Delworth (ed.). *Dealing with the Behavioral and Psychological Problems of Students.*
New Directions for Student Services, no. 45. San Francisco: Jossey-Bass, Spring 1989.

backgrounds are to learn together, standard orientation programs may not be enough. In order for students to realize all of the benefits of learning together in a multicultural community, they must first receive some instruction on how to interact appropriately with one another.

Multicultural Awareness

Minority students cannot all be viewed as having the same cultural characteristics, as coming from the same social or economic backgrounds, or as having the same responses to the same higher education experience (Webster, Sedlacek, and Miyares, 1979). Black, Hispanic, Asian-American, and Native American students may differ from one another in their responses to the educational environment, and they may have different responses from those of white students. Students within a minority group may also have different experiences at different institutions (Patterson, Sedlacek, and Perry, 1984). Between students of each minority subgroup there are differing values, educational backgrounds, and attitudes, which stem from such variables as whether the students grew up in urban or rural environments, whether they are the first persons from their family to go to college, whether they were born in America, and whether they have come from economically well-off or from disadvantaged families. In the AISP model, the staff members responsible for assessing the student, and thus for moving the student into other levels of assessment or intervention, must be trained sufficiently about multicultural differences in order to make knowledgeable assessments.

Multicultural awareness training can be provided to the student services staff at the same time that the AISP model's three student categories are explained. It would be more challenging to provide such training to the faculty, the cultural center, the recreational center, academic advisers, and others who also interact with students. At large, decentralized institutions, multicultural training of faculty and other academic staff members can and should be done, but it requires tremendous commitment.

Multicultural awareness training can be provided to residence-hall staff, peer counselors, tutors, and other staff members working with minority students; however, it is difficult to impart the experience required to differentiate between a minority student's responding appropriately to the environment and his or her exhibiting symptoms of a more serious nature. Fleming (1984, pp. 168–169) describes the experience of black men at predominantly white universities as being frustrating, their aspirations defeated in a "context of falling grades in the critical major subjects, diminishing feelings of intellectual ability, declining social adjustment, and losses in perceived energy level suggestive of emotional strain." Could a well-trained, less-experienced staff member, such as a residence-hall worker (who might also be a student) be astute enough to recognize when the student situation requires a referral?

Two recent tragic events might be illustrative here. On June 12, 1985, Edmund Perry was shot and killed just two months before starting classes at Stanford, where he would have received a scholarship. He was allegedly attempting to mug a police officer. Perry, who was a graduate of Phillips Exeter Academy, an elite prep school, was by all accounts bright, disciplined, articulate, confident, ambitious, and proud of his cultural heritage. He had no criminal record, but during his senior year at Exeter he seemed to become more militant, more willing to take risks such as sneaking out of the dorm at night, much more sensitive to racial issues, and more involved in the drug subculture (Anson, 1987).

Though some of Perry's friends thought that he was becoming increasingly more distressed, the three part-time house parents who staffed Perry's thirty-six-member dorm seemed unaware of his difficulties. In hindsight it seems quite possible that Edmund Perry was experiencing great emotional difficulty with reconciling his success in a predominantly white environment with his personal background as a young black from Harlem. In fact, while many of his friends and teachers overlooked his behavior or were intimidated by it, at least one teacher recommended counseling (Anson, 1987).

The second distressing example is that of Jose Razo, who was a freshman at Harvard in fall 1985, but who confessed to a series of armed robberies that occurred across an almost two-year period during college vacations. According to a newspaper account, Razo lived in a dormitory to which student athletes were frequently assigned, seemed popular, and seemed to be adjusting well to his college environment. Other than the gifts to his family purchased with the money from the robberies, there seemed to be only a few clues to the turmoil he may have been experiencing while trying to reconcile his cultural background with his desire to succeed at Harvard. Gradually, Razo seemed to become more concerned with his Mexican heritage, giving up his fashionable clothes to don the baggy pants, T-shirt, pointed black shoes, and bandana of the *cholo* (Lindsey, 1987). It is difficult to determine whether Razo's behavior at Harvard caused any concern, because the changes were subtle, and as with Perry's behavior, there were touchy racial overtones that may have caused general discomfort and a desire to avoid the issue.

Minority Students and the AISP Model

This discussion does not attempt to determine whether the AISP model would have somehow intervened to the benefit of these two young men. The information that has been provided is sketchy, and there is no implication that anyone behaved unprofessionally or otherwise inappropriately. The point is that staff and faculty members, if properly trained, can fit each example into one or more of the model's three general categories of student behavior. For minority students, the usefulness of the AISP model depends on the ability of the staff and faculty to distinguish between behavior resulting from culture shock and behavior indicative of other difficulties. After all, college should be a time of tremendous personal development and intellectual challenge, with some personal difficulty to be anticipated. Mental health professionals and other student services staff members must be able to describe indicators of inappropriate behavior for minority students in order to make useful assessments. The staff and faculty must also be sensitive to whether the behavior is culturally appropriate. For instance, is giving up conventional clothes and dressing like a *cholo* at Harvard culturally appropriate from a Hispanic perspective? Or is greater militancy toward racial issues by a black student seen as understandable behavior from the perspective of other blacks? If assessments of minority students are to be effective in the AISP model, the faculty and staff must have a set of clearly defined parameters outlining both predictable and more problematic behavior from a culturally appropriate point of view.

The strength of the AISP model is that while the staff and faculty and respective supervisors perform the assessment of the student and make referrals to appropriate agencies, the campus intervention team assumes responsibility for following up to make certain that the referral is working. Harried younger workers and faculty members, who may not often have the opportunity to work with an individual student, are spared having to keep track of a student. In this way the delivery of potentially crucial services to students becomes an institutional concern.

For minority students who generally avoid established support facilities such as counseling services (Livingston and Stewart, 1987) the campus intervention team can provide additional incentive to use available services. Since the staff and faculty frequently do not know if a referral has been successful, the team can serve as a valuable bridge, providing useful information about completed referrals. And if a student refuses the referral or leaves the campus, the team can still persist in its follow up.

In the case of minority students attending predominantly a white institution, the staff performing the assessments and the campus intervention team should focus on the difference between expected adjustment issues and more alarming behavior. This can sometimes prove quite complicated and involve judgments that are rather intuitive in nature. To classify a minority student as "disturbing" is a fairly clear-cut procedure because the characteristics of disturbing students include disturbing the campus environment and not exhibiting distinct indicators of psychological disturbance. The category of disturbed student, however, is more difficult to apply because the assessment must be based on the intensity of the signs of disturbance, and the signs can vary widely. After all, it is difficult to define being *out of sync* in the context of different cultural perspectives.

As has been pointed out earlier, the most common kind of disturbances are related to stress and the anxieties associated with adjusting a new environment. In the case of some minority students attending a predominantly white campus, the gulf between their previous life experience and their new environment may be so great that they become unhappy, depressed, and disoriented for long periods of time. In the absence of extreme behavior, such as withdrawal or depression, or inappropriate behaviors in public, such as substance abuse, there is no clear-cut rule about when to intervene. This is especially true when adjustment difficulties are suspected, since everyone experiences these difficulties to one degree or another. Decisions about when to intervene and how to intervene must be made with sensitivity to cultural differences. For example, an Asian-American student's response to an intervention depends not only on the form of the intervention and the person delivering the intervention but also on the amount of acculturation the student has undergone and the sensitivity of the staff person performing the assessment. When a faculty member recommends a visit to the counseling center, it is not difficult to imagine that a third- or fourth-generation Asian-American student might have an entirely different response from that of a recent immigrant.

It is very helpful to include other relevant persons in the campus intervention team, such as an adviser who sees many minority students or the director of the university support program or the manager of the cultural center. The AISP model is most effective when an effort is made to address the ambiguities of racial interaction in the campus environment. Though institutions of higher education seek or are forced to have greater diversity in their enrollment, the presumption seems to be that persons from diverse backgrounds will somehow know how to get along in the new environment. Even orientation programs for minority students portray the university as a fixed environment and advocate that the students adapt themselves to it. But the reality is that through their very presence on a campus, minority students bring change to the environment, change to which everyone in the environment must adapt.

Colleges and universities serving a diverse student body must develop methods to educate all students about how to interact appropriately with one another. Except in a few unique settings, it makes no sense to presume that black, Hispanic, Asian-American, Native American, and white students have developed the skills necessary for working with one another. For many students, their first significant intercultural experience will occur when they go off to college, and for some students, positive interracial experiences are important in their decisions to remain enrolled

(Bennett, 1984). When working with students after an incident involving a racial slur, for instance, there will be those who feel the slur was not intended maliciously and in fact was of little significance. Other students, however, may react very adversely to the slur and in some way or another disturb the campus environment. In the AISP model, the task of assessment and providing services to students is much easier, since the atmosphere is one in which everyone has a clear idea of what constitutes inappropriate interracial behavior and why.

The AISP model forces institutions to be responsive to the reality that different kinds of students may react differently to campus conditions. In a time when college campuses are becoming more diverse, it is appropriate that the student services staff and the faculty be trained in cultural sensitivity and be knowledgeable about the different ways students may respond to the campus environment. Also, since it is well known that many minority students hesitate to use support facilities such as counseling services, the campus intervention team provides institutional follow up, which often prevents a student from "falling through the cracks." Finally, implicit in the AISP model is the understanding that the response of every student to the campus environment should be of concern not only to a few student services specialists but to the entire campus community.

References

Anson, R. S. *Best Intentions: The Education and Killing of Edmund Perry.* New York: Random House, 1987.

Bennett, C. "Interracial Contact Experience and Attrition Among Black Undergraduates at a Predominantly White University." *Theory and Research in Social Education,* 1984, *12* (2), 19–47.

Christoffel, P. "Minority Student Access and Retention: A Review." In *Research and Development Update.* New York: College Entrance Examination Board, October 1986.

Fleming, J. *Blacks in College: A Comparative Study of Students' Success in Black and in White Institutions.* San Francisco: Jossey-Bass, 1984.

Lindsey, R. "Worlds in Collision: From Barrio to Harvard to Jail." *New York Times,* July 26, 1987, Sec. 1, p. 20.

Livingston, M. D., and Stewart, M. A. "Minority Students on a White Campus: Perception Is Truth." *NASPA Journal,* 1987, *24* (3), 39–49.

Patterson, A. M., Sedlacek, W. E., and Perry, F. W. "Perceptions of Blacks and Hispanics in Two Campus Environments." *Journal of College Student Personnel,* 1984, *25* (6), 513–518.

Webster, D. W., Sedlacek, W. E., and Miyares, J. "A Comparison of Problems Perceived by Minority and White University Students." *Journal of College Student Personnel,* 1979, *20* (2), 165–170.

Paul Shang is director of the Help for Education and Life Planning Center (HELP Center) at Colorado State University. In addition to advising students in the University's Open Option academic program, the HELP Center coordinates orientation programs, career development workshops, and support for the faculty's scholastic standards review.

Would the AISP model work for the college student-athlete?
A brief case study suggests possibilities and raises issues.

Applying the AISP Model to the College Student-Athlete

James J. Rhatigan

One of the primary responsibilities of student affairs administrations is to recognize student issues and problems and to find ways of resolving them. Scholars sometimes suggest helpful approaches, and the Assessment-Intervention of Student Problems (AISP) model is but one example of these. Of course, the test of any model is how well it works. In this section an attempt is made to consider the student-athlete, an identifiable subpopulation on most campuses, to see how or whether the AISP model might apply.

A case study of an issue involving student-athletes in a residence hall will serve as a point of departure: Art and Bob, two members of the college's successful football program, had vandalized the lounge on the floor of the residence hall where they both lived. The incident occurred late in the evening after the last game of the season, a game that assured the college of the league title. Damage to the lounge included broken furniture, torn cushions, and holes punched in one wall by the fist of one or both of the players. The resident adviser who had heard the noise and discovered the mayhem asserted that both players appeared to be very drunk. Both students responded to the adviser's admonitions, so the campus police were not called.

A closer investigation of the matter revealed that Art was a successful

U. Delworth (ed.). *Dealing with the Behavioral and Psychological Problems of Students.*
New Directions for Student Services, no. 45. San Francisco: Jossey-Bass, Spring 1989.

running back, immature but responsive to authority, popular with men and women students, academically adequate, and a hero of the last game of the season. Art admitted later that he had had too much alcohol.

Bob was a tackle who had lost his starting position during the third game. Bob's coach had told him that a poor attitude and lack of effort were the reasons. Bob had been shocked and felt that he had been treated unfairly. He wondered if his being black had been a factor in the decision of his new coach. By the sixth game he was moved even lower in the depth chart for his position.

Bob is not popular among the other students, cultivating a fearsome presence. His 275-pound frame showed the scars of long years in the football trenches. He enjoyed the company of a handful of close friends who were linemen on the team.

What cannot be generally seen is the depth of the hurt that Bob felt. His classroom attitude and performance were negatively affected. He could not bring himself to quit the team and he would not talk about his problems because he felt too humiliated. Bob's friends did not suspect the depth of his feelings.

The reader may classify Art as a disturbing student (type A in the model). Perhaps, but not certainly, Bob can be described as a disturbed/disturbing student.

If the AISP model had been used on the campus, how would it have worked in this case? Does the model enjoy any particular efficacy for subpopulations like student-athletes? One way to decide is by working through the case hypothetically.

We must first determine how an initial assessment of the two students should have been made. This was a seemingly straightforward case of vandalism in a residence hall, where the perpetrators have been caught. On most campuses some weight would be given to the student's history of behavior on the halls, and a fair-minded judicial board would want to hear the student's version of what had taken place. But it is doubtful that any real assessment of motivation or a player's emotional state would have been made. This lack of assessment would probably not be too serious in Art's case, but it might make all the difference to Bob's.

Probably the residence assistant or the hall director would make the initial assessment and refer the students to the judicial process. These typically are entry-level people. Under normal circumstances, neither of them would understand Bob's circumstance. On the contrary, they would probably view him as a sullen presence in the halls.

Since both players were found at the scene, and neither could recall who had done what to the lounge, the appropriate judicial source would probably hand down some sort of disciplinary ruling. Nothing suggests that the two would receive differential treatment.

A normal intervention would consist of the players' paying for damages and being placed on some sort of probation. They might also be removed from the hall. The disciplinary decision in this case would probably miss the psychological motivations of the two players.

Let us carry this hypothetical discipline process even further. Because the assessment step was weak, the entire process was affected. There was appropriate punishment, but there was no rehabilitative or redemptive feature in the disciplinary decision. A campus intervention team would probably not involve itself in this seemingly straightforward case of vandalism in the residence halls. But let us assume that at some point the campus intervention team did intervene. To make any judgment (and recommendation), the team would have to decide (1) whether Bob's actions had been motivated by self-pity, which may be understandable but does not justify further intervention; (2) whether Bob's actions signal an emerging pathology of unknown dimensions; or (3) whether he had been treated unjustly. Though the three possibilities are not mutually exclusive, of course, any real evidence that (3) is a possibility brings up issues for the campus intervention team that are more complicated and that carry greater potential consequences than would have been predicted from the original incident. But how would a team learn that the third possibility had actually occurred? Certainly not from Bob. Does this dilemma suggest the impracticality of the model, or does it suggest the need for it?

On a growing number of campuses there are persons described as academic advisers of athletes. They may serve part time or full time in this role, but when the position exists on a campus, the intervention model for athletes brightens considerably. These advisers are capable of serving as experts on the problems and issues of the student-athlete. Though their role is often one of advocacy, they are nonetheless well equipped to explain impartially the world of athletics to the rest of the campus.

An academic adviser for athletes can serve in an advisory role for a campus intervention team. Student-athletes know that their advisers are their advocates; certainly the good ones befriend many athletes who need someone to confide in. A well-informed campus intervention team is in an excellent position to help faculty and administrative personnel understand the unique pressures of the student-athlete. When specific problems surface, a general sensitivity and understanding are already in place on the campus.

On many campuses the perception of the college student-athlete is little more than a stereotype. He or she is often seen as pampered, with every transgression excused or covered up. There is another view (Rhatigan, 1984) that suggests nearly the opposite idea, that the system of higher education often treats these men and women roughly. The campus intervention team can work to reduce stereotypes and to reevaluate campus rules and procedures that hurt student-athletes.

The campus intervention team should contain a core of regular members, with others added according to their understanding of one or more campus subpopulations. The exact role a team plays requires further clarification. Does it serve as investigator, evaluator, referee, consultant, arbiter, or monitor? Does it serve as an educational resource for the campus? Does the team seek only to influence, or does it look for bureaucratic decision-making power of some sort? A policy function seems implicit in reviewing a team's potential, but no policy function is explicitly indicated in the model.

In the case example discussed in this chapter the campus intervention team would have to decide what its role would be if it reviewed the case of Bob and found that greater accountability on the part of the athletic department was required. It may find that other athletes suspect prejudicial or unfair treatment on the part of Bob's coach. The ability of a team to dig out such information is a potential strength of great importance to any campus.

On large campuses it may be necessary to have several intervention teams. In 1985 one prestigious university had to review nearly fifteen hundred judicial cases in its residence-hall system alone. A single campus intervention team would be impractical in this sort of environment. A parent team could be established to serve as a consulting resource and as a training vehicle for a number of intervention teams. Each residence-hall complex, for example, could have an intervention team of its own. The campus intervention team might involve itself in complex cases or in cases of campuswide significance, otherwise choosing to serve in less direct ways. Certainly it would play the role of overseer for the larger campus.

The AISP model appears to have enough flexibility to permit a modest program for any campus that might be interested. The scope of the model can be broadened as experience deems appropriate. Specialty teams can serve a very useful purpose, as in the case of the college student-athlete. The model encourages this sort of exploration and experimentation.

A policy role for the campus intervention team might well emerge as the team's reputation increases. An experienced team might conclude that certain campus practices produce negative consequences, as demonstrated by the kinds of cases the team confronts. The campus intervention team seems ideally suited for suggesting new or modified policies, or for working toward the elimination of practices that damage the campus environment.

The AISP model seems worthy of any student affairs practitioner's attention. It suggests one way for a campus to approach unproductive or unhealthy student behavior in a more thorough and thoughtful manner than has been the case on many campuses. Although the model has an individual focus, it may eventually yield dividends that will benefit the campus as a whole.

Reference

Rhatigan, J. J. "Serving Two Masters: The Plight of the College Student-Athlete." In A. Shriberg and F. Brodzinski (eds.), *Rethinking Services for College Athletes*. New Directions for Student Services, no. 28. San Francisco: Jossey-Bass, 1984.

James J. Rhatigan is vice-president for student affairs and dean of students at Wichita State University. He has been involved for twenty-five years in professional issues and activities of concern to campus administrators in student affairs.

The AISP model will prove valuable when used with commuter students. However, it may be necessary to adapt the model to more closely reflect the campus environment and types of students.

The AISP Model: Use with Commuter Students

Susan J. Eklund-Leen

The Assessment-Intervention of Student Problems (AISP) model does indeed offer each practitioner a vehicle through which he or she can categorize student behavior problems. As each person reads this model many examples will come to mind. The ease with which this model can assess behavior makes it seem too good to be true.

No matter which type of student (traditional, nontraditional, commuter, resident) characterizes a campus, the practitioner can readily assess students through those behaviors witnessed. However, this model works best with traditional students at a predominately residential campus, where behavior in several environments can easily be observed. Commuter students may exhibit totally appropriate behavior while attending classes or using campus facilities, but they may demonstrate disturbed or disturbing behavior while at home or in other environments. The AISP model cannot be used to its fullest potential when behaviors are not exhibited in the campus environment or when no reporting mechanisms can be created.

The AISP model can be quite helpful when commuter students who experience problems are quite well known to the faculty and staff. Students active in student organizations, theater, or sports, and students with on-campus jobs seem to be much more visible to the faculty and staff.

U. Delworth (ed.). *Dealing with the Behavioral and Psychological Problems of Students.*
New Directions for Student Services, no. 45. San Francisco: Jossey-Bass, Spring 1989.

These students spend more time on campus and tend to know at least one faculty member or professional staff member quite well. Whenever a campus intervention team is convened to evaluate a commuter student's behavior, it should, whenever possible, include the staff member who interacts most closely with the student. This staff member could be a work supervisor, club adviser, counselor, or academic adviser.

Case example: Anne was a forty-year-old woman who had recently begun her college education. Anne performed adequately academically, made friends easily, became involved in activities, and spent a great deal of time on campus. Each term she registered for sixteen or seventeen credit hours but eventually dropped one or two courses. Her explanation each time was that she was too busy with all of her other responsibilities and cocurricular activities.

Though this profile may seem like the picture of a perfectly healthy student who only needs to learn time management skills, the truth was that Anne was trying to escape her unhappiness at home by pursuing her education. The effects of the psychological abuse she was suffering at home interfered with everything Anne tried to do.

Dropping courses really resulted from a combination of Anne's not being able to study at home because of her husband's interference and her consequent inability to trust and interact with men. Anne always dropped courses that were taught by men.

Without the additional information about Anne's home life and distrust of men, no one on campus could adequately help her develop necessary coping skills, assist her with finding professional help, or provide support for Anne to complete her degree. Anne's only hope for assistance through the college could come when she honestly faced and explained her problems.

Categorizing Anne according to the AISP model would place her as a type A-B 3 disturbed student. Anne's distrust of men did have an outward focus, her symptoms, which had persisted throughout her marriage, were long-standing, and she showed no real change in her behavior. Only through appropriate counseling and action could Anne hope to resolve her problems.

No matter which persons serve on the campus intervention team, they must always remember that their goal is to help the student develop appropriate behaviors, which integrate him or her into campus life. However, they should realize that they may not be able to find or influence the root cause for the inappropriate behavior if the cause is external to the campus and the student refuses to discuss his or her problem.

Case example: Arnie was a student who was difficult to assess. He had been enrolled part time for nearly eight years. Arnie had tried unsuccessfully to be accepted by other students through membership in nearly every club on campus. He floated from club to club, hoping to be appointed as the club's representative to student government, which he believed would elevate his status on campus. During club meetings Arnie filibustered about inappropriate and unimportant topics. Other members dreaded listening to him, and the chair almost never permitted Arnie to speak.

After having joined nearly every organization, Arnie stumbled on one that was affiliated with a support group for handicapped students. With the help of the support-group leader Arnie learned that he had a learning disability that prevented him from distinguishing between relevant and irrelevant information. The diagnosis of his learning disability would never have occurred without Arnie's becoming involved in this student organization's support group.

Earlier Arnie had been labeled a know-it-all who tried to gain attention by voicing his opinion on every issue. After the diagnosis his behavior could still be annoying to other students, but he could develop skills to deal with his learning disability. Not only could Arnie begin to relate in a more acceptable fashion but he could also become a better student.

When applying the AISP model, Arnie could be categorized as a disturbed/disturbing student. His desire to manipulate others through his filibustering techniques at meetings was not entirely intentional, but it did qualify Arnie as a type B disturbing student. He also exhibited several of the general characteristics of a disturbing student. Arnie also fit into the category of a type A-B 3 disturbed student. His learning disability was a known and long-standing cause of his behavior. Though Arnie did not appear to be angry, his inappropriate behavior and his fixation on becoming a representative of student government did qualify him as a type A-B 3 disturbed student. Combining these, Arnie's category was type A-B 3 disturbed/type B disturbing.

When using the AISP model, the categorization of disturbing students into type A (immature and impulsive) and type B (controlling and manipulative) could clarify as well as confuse. Type A behavior is more overt than the type B behavior. Type A students usually behave in a manner that is easily classified. However, type B disturbing students may be harder to categorize.

The manipulating and controlling behavior of the type B disturbing student may be developed to such an extent that members of a campus intervention team at a commuter campus may not easily recognize that a problem exists. A charming, well-spoken student who expresses what seems to be sincere intentions could easily gain recognition and a position of authority in a student organization. This student may seem like a natural leader, and his or her actual motivation may never become apparent. Unfortunately, the type B disturbing behavior may be unknowingly reinforced when this student is seen in limited settings.

The categories of type A disturbed student (inward focus) and type B disturbed student (outward focus) may appear easy to recognize and distinguish. But categorizing commuter students as disturbed or disturbed/disturbing presents the greatest challenge to practitioners at commuter campuses. Symptoms may be noticed, but the causes of disturbed behavior may never be revealed by the student. Consequently, appropriate intervention may not be possible if the student decides to keep confidential significant events from his or her past. Practitioners who notice disturbed behavior should attempt to create a situation that is safe enough to allow the student to talk about himself or herself.

Subtleties in behavior will make identification more difficult in many situations. The student affairs practitioner must be as observant as possible and evaluate all aspects of behavior. Practitioners at urban, commuter campuses can benefit from using the AISP model. It is composed in simple terms, thus making it not only easy to use but also easy to learn for the professional staff, faculty, and support staff. All college employees who interact closely with students can benefit from learning the AISP model.

However, one caution must be noted: The behavior of commuter students while on campus is really seen in isolation. Behavior at home and at work is just as important as behavior while in class or on campus. The opportunity to witness student behavior in all life situations is not possible at an urban commuter campus. At best, the AISP model can only provide an incomplete picture of behavior if the student is not willing to provide the missing pieces.

Like every theory or model, the AISP model is not perfect for all campuses. Understanding the model in its entirety, recognizing its limitations for use at different types of campuses, and adapting the model to more closely fit a particular campus and type of student will allow each practitioner to use this model most appropriately. No matter what the circumstances, the AISP model can prove beneficial because of its simplicity and its attempt to integrate many functions that all too often operate in isolation.

Susan J. Eklund-Leen is director of student activities for Sinclair Community College in Dayton, Ohio. She has held numerous positions for the Ohio College Personnel Association and has served as a member at large for the American College Personnel Association.

Clarity and coordination are key ingredients in the AISP model. Both are necessary for effective implementation.

Closing Notes

Ursula Delworth

It has been humbling, frustrating at times, and immensely rewarding to see a concept that was originally developed for a three-hour workshop grow into a model that is taken seriously by the student affairs profession. I am fortunate in having colleagues who, in these pages, have explored how the model relates to their own worlds of practice, and who have found much in it to recommend.

I am impressed by Ragle and Justice's articulation of the developmental dimensions of the judicial system and their excellent examples of how these relate to disturbing students. This dimension also has potential for work with some disturbed/disturbing students. However, as Brown and DeCoster note, many of the difficulties these students experience are of a more profound and highly remedial nature.

McKinley and Dworkin's call for a broader and more integrated institutional response to disturbed students is a vital message. As they note, emotional distress does not necessarily mean that a student cannot perform well in the classroom. The ecological perspective they advocate has great potential for addressing the needs of this particular group of students.

My colleagues also raise important questions. Rhatigan is concerned with the policy role of the campus intervention team. Though the role is implicit, it is not spelled out. As Rhatigan notes, an experienced team is in an excellent position to evaluate campus policies and procedures.

U. Delworth (ed.). *Dealing with the Behavioral and Psychological Problems of Students.*
New Directions for Student Services, no. 45. San Francisco: Jossey-Bass, Spring 1989.

Thus some sort of policy involvement appears both feasible and useful. Exactly what form this involvement should take is best determined by each campus.

Comments by Eklund-Leen and Shang emphasize the difficulties in conceptualizing a model that is effective on all types of campuses and for all students. As Eklund-Leen notes, a commuter student's behavior on campus may be only a small sample of his or her total pattern of behavior, thus making assessment in the Assessment-Intervention of Student Problems (AISP) model much more difficult. Shang warns us that the usefulness of the model depends on the ability of staff members to distinguish between behavior that is "normal" for someone in a strange and hostile environment and behavior that is indicative of greater difficulties. Indeed, the AISP model is probably most directly relevant to a residential campus and traditional-age white students. I am heartened that both Shang and Eklund-Leen see possibilities for expansion beyond this base.

Sandeen raises a number of important issues regarding the cost-effectiveness of the model, and these cannot be easily answered. The specter of yet another mechanism, the campus intervention team, which would tie up valuable personnel in frequent meetings, is a troubling one. The model requires this kind of effort, however, in order to succeed. Over time, as with any successful enterprise, the effort expended and hours needed should decrease, as personnel become familiar with procedures. And on many campuses we are currently spending a good deal of time dealing as separate agencies with the same students.

In the end, the AISP model is an attempt to find the most effective and humane manner in which to deal with students who are in pain or are causing difficulties on campus. And here, after a volume full of *d*'s (disturbed, disturbing, and disturbed/disturbing), I have come to believe that some answers can be found in the *c*'s. The words *clarity* and *coordination* appear a number of times in Sandeen's chapter. These two words probably summarize best the values orientation of the model. They are worth a bit more exploration.

Clarity is a key ingredient in the AISP model, which attempts to present ideas and guidelines in a straightforward manner, avoiding professional jargon. The model strives for inclusiveness through clarity; that is, students who are experiencing internal or external problems require the focused attention of the institutional staff at all levels. Only a simple, clear model will allow understanding and practice by a diverse group of professionals.

Coordination builds on this theme of inclusiveness, and asserts that we serve students better when we serve them in an integrated, cooperative manner. The model leaves no room for agencies or personnel who wish to work in a private and uncooperative manner. Issues such as confidentiality and due process must be addressed explicitly in using the AISP model, but they must not be allowed to become barriers to appropriate concern and involvement.

More important than some of the specifics is that this model can really offer an affirmation of the core values of clarity and coordination. To the extent that this potential is realized, our students and our institutions will be better served.

Ursula Delworth is a student affairs professional and psychologist who is currently a professor in the Department of Psychological and Quantitative Foundations of Education, The University of Iowa.

Index